Without Burnt Offerings

ALGERNON D. BLACK

WITHOUT BURNT OFFERINGS

Ceremonies of Humanism

"Without Burnt Offerings" by Algernon D. Black. ISBN 978-0-9897323-5-2.

Manufactured in the United States of America Printed in the United States of America

Acknowledgment is made to the following for permission to quote material: The Macmillan Publishing Co., Inc., The Macmillan Company of Canada Limited, Macmillan, London and Basingstoke, and Mrs. I. Wise: From *Collected Poems* by James Stephens. Copyright 1938 by Macmillan Publishing Co. Inc. Reprinted by permission. Charles Scribner's Sons and Constable & Co. Ltd.: "To W.P." from *Poems* by George Santayana. Copyright 1923 Charles Scribner's Sons; renewal 1951 George Santayana. Reprinted by permission.

To John Lovejoy Elliott
1869-1942

---

*Leader of the New York Society for Ethical Culture
and Member of the Fraternity of Leaders of the
American Ethical Union, Ethics Teacher and Head
of the Department of Ethics of the Ethical Culture
Schools, Social Worker and Founder and Headworker
of the Hudson Guild Neighborhood House, through
half a century he exemplified the best in the religious
leadership of a "Ministry to Man." With Felix Adler,
in his teaching and his leadership in the cause of
freedom and equality he expressed the best in the
prophetic tradition. He loved people and he
lived the ethics he taught.*

Acknowledgments

This book has grown out of experiences with the lives of countless individuals and families over a period of almost fifty years. In some instances it has been possible to include their names, and in some situations, with their permission, it has been possible to include actual quotations from their spoken and written words.

To Ms. Ginal Calkins, my most able assistant, I am especially indebted for critical judgment, sympathetic understanding, and patience, and for her skill in assembling and organizing the many selections which are included in the text. I wish also to thank Ms. Danielle Woerner for her production and preparation of the manuscript and for many valuable suggestions.

William T. Stone, a distinguished journalist and a lifelong friend, has generously taken time out of a busy life to read the manuscript and offer the benefit of his literary judgment. No thanks can adequately express my debt to the editor, Merrill Pollack of The Viking Press, who has given extra time and painstaking attention to weeding out my grammatical errors and evaluating my selections. The collaboration with him has been a pleasant and stimulating and constructive experience.

I would be remiss indeed if I did not express my appreciation to the Leaders and members of the Ethical Culture Movement, whose freedom of spirit and independence of thought in times of excessive conformity have been a constant source of nourishment and inspiration.

Last, but not least, I wish to express my thanks to my wife, Elinor Goldmark Black, for her encouragement and her literary judgment; she has always been ready to rephrase or rearrange the words and sentences and structure to be sure that the book is true to the meaning I intended to convey.

Contents

MEMORIAL
SERVICES

INVOCATIONS

Foreword

It is strange for me to have written this book. My interest and work have been primarily as a teacher, social worker, and activist for social change. Ceremonies had always seemed to me to be a survival of traditional rituals based on the myths and creeds of the old religions of supernaturalism. I regarded them as external to the real struggles of life, decorative, empty forms, signs of human weakness. How could ceremonies be part of Humanism? How could I write about them?

My first experiences came through calls at times of death. When the Leaders of the Ethical Societies were called for funerals or memorial services, they thought that I, as a young assistant, should begin to understand the needs of the bereaved and how the philosophy of Ethical Humanism might help. At times the Leaders asked me to participate, especially at the cemetery. It was an aid to them and difficult for me, but a valuable part of my training.

As I worked with young people, some couples indicated that they would like me to officiate at their weddings. When I became a Leader with legal authorization to function on such occasions, I felt the challenge of making such weddings honest and beautiful and meaningful experiences. The variety of situations in which young people came to the Society at the time of marriage was interesting, exciting, and challenging. One had to try to be fresh and original and relevant to their needs.

Then came the invitations to speak at graduations and commence-

i

ments and "recognition" days. How to make these occasions meaning-ful in relation to the basic questions of life purpose and human values? How to make the experience one which would go beyond mere formality, something which the young could share with each other, with parents and teachers and friends? I tried to make each one a teaching and learning experience.

When I was called to name a baby, that was the last thing I wanted to do. Was my function to invoke the protection of God or to pretend that Humanism could assure a soul and salvation to the newborn? The new baby would not know what was going on. What value could this ceremony have?

As I experienced these ceremonies, the preparation for them, and the reactions of people, old and young, of every variety of religious and nonreligious background, I began to appreciate their meaning and value. I began to see that there was a wisdom in some of the traditional practices of religion even though I differed with their dogmatic theological doctrines, their mythology and fixed, repetitious,
symbolic, and mystical basis. In the crises of life, both the joyous and the sad and tragic moments, the familiar association with words and symbols and rituals brought stability and control at times when emotions and anxieties were disturbing.

I began to realize that through ceremonies Humanism could help people face difficulty and crisis. Ceremonies could be part of the spirit of Humanism. They could offer ways of celebrating life which would be creative and loving, which could nourish the inner life of human beings with dignity, honesty, and beauty. They might help people live with greater meaning and courage.

So my ideas about the value and meaning of ceremonies underwent a change. I realized that in a pre-scientific age it was natural for human beings to create some plausible explanations out of their needs for security and protection. In their myths were explanations of why the winds blow, why the sun and moon come and go, why the tides rise and fall, why there is a season when crops grow and lambs are born, and a season when birds fly south. Human beings in all cultures have tried to explain the mysteries of birth and death. The explanations reveal an underlying similarity, despite the differences of language and ways of life. The answers have been found in a world of spirits in the earth and waters and heavenly bodies, spirits in wind, lightning, and thunder, and in all living things. The problem was to make certain that these spirits were friendly or at least not hostile, to win their favor for protection and fertility and survival. They could assure success in hunting and fishing. In a pastoral society they could assure lambs, and in an agricultural society, crops. Beyond this, they could assure victory against enemies and safety with neighbors. They were to be appeased when they were angry and destructive in storms and earthquakes, in floods and droughts, in famine, plague, and pestilence. Whatever the formulation of beliefs and myths, it was through ceremonies, symbols, and rituals that human beings dealt with the spirit world.

Some of the ceremonies had to do with the community's undertakings. At the beginning of a task, the ceremony was a way of asking for help, and at the end it was a way of expressing thanks. Similarly, when people undertook an expedition, exploration, or war, they felt the need to invoke the spirits. Ceremonies were also ways of commemorating the birth, death, and achievements of a great warrior, ruler, or holy man. These were community occasions, but there were also ceremonies to celebrate and help on occasions of personal importance: the birth of a child in the family; the arrival of puberty, when boy becomes man and girl becomes woman. These events marked a change in status and role, the assumption of responsibilities and participation in adult life. Similarly, ceremonies celebrated the change from single to marital status and the assumption of responsibilities of a family and a home. Finally, with the end of a life, ceremonies expressed grief and assured an afterlife in the world of the dead. The living performed certain duties to the dead, so that they were protected from any hurt the dead might do to the living. These were all occasions for ceremonies which would assure protection and support, health and achievement and fertility. In these rituals, anthropologists have seen practices which met universal human needs beyond the many cultural differences of tribal societies. They have called these rituals the "rites of passage."

It is important that we who live in the twentieth century remember the long struggle of human beings to survive and to make sense out of their natural environment. The problem for us now is to understand not only the principles and laws of our natural environment but also those of our human environment. If we undertake this seriously, we must make more of an effort to understand ourselves, the laws of our own organism—physiological, mental, emotional, aesthetic, ethical, and spiritual. Even if we no longer believe the ancient myths and creeds, or perform the traditional rituals, we should ask if there is any reality in what might be termed man's spiritual nature.

MAN'S SPIRITUAL NEED

The spiritual nature manifests itself in certain tendencies in man. Is it not true that most men at certain moments in their lives are aware of a need within them for something more than the satisfaction that they derive from eating, drinking, sleeping, breeding, and the fulfillment of immediate desire? Is it not true that most men want to think of themselves as more than animal? For many, that extra something beyond physical levels may be satisfied by intellectual or aesthetic experiences. But most men appear to hunger for something that goes beyond even these.

Man's spiritual nature is also evident in the widespread tendency to seek a reality deeper than the reality he knows through his senses. Man is not satisfied that he can rely completely on the external sources of his perceptions, nor is he satisfied that he can trust his own sense organs completely. There is a transient and temporary aspect to the reality he knows through his senses. He longs for something permanent and changeless, less subjective and subject to his own errors.

All men share with others the external world they experience and live in. But every man lives also in a private world of his own personal experience, his wishes and dreams of the self he would like to be and the life he would like to live and the world he would like to live in.

Man longs for freedom and the power to master the forces that play upon him. His passion for freedom makes him long to transcend the bonds of the chemistry and the instinctive patterns of his own physical nature. He hungers for growth and fulfillment of his individual unique possibilities. But he also longs for security, for identity with some larger reality of which he can be a meaningful part. He wishes to be part of a larger process. He would gladly bind himself with the values that give life its greatest meaning.

Man longs to know that what he values as good and true and beautiful is grounded in the nature of things, that his values and his struggle for a better life are validated in nature, and that his life has meaning not only for himself and his fellows and the generations to come, but also in some larger context of the universe.

WHAT RELIGION CONTRIBUTES

These are some of the characteristics of human beings the world over. They appear in individuals and in groups in ways for which there is no single explanation. They are an expression of deep hungers of the human spirit. They have brought forth endless questioning and all the varieties of answers that we know as the philosophies and the religions of humankind. And it is doubtless true that this aspect of man's life will be evident in endless seeking as long as he lives on this earth.

The spiritual need of man has expressed itself in traditional religions. In the Western world the interpretations of life by Judaism, Christianity, and Islam have emphasized the dualistic approach. Most of the churches have taught a concept of spiritual reality that has to do with God, the supernatural, another world, a realm of divinity and sacredness, as over against the natural world, the material and secular realm of being. Just as God is the soul of the universe, so man himself is conceived of dualistically, as body and soul, flesh and spirit.

Who would dare to say that men have not been helped in their spiritual needs by this vision of life? For it has given men hope and faith that they are more than animal and that there is more to life than the satisfaction of immediate desire. It has given them a belief in a reality absolute, changeless, and eternal. Insofar as men have believed in this, they have felt a personal dignity, a support from a power making for righteousness, an inevitable victory for their vision of a better life and a better world. No doubt it has contributed much to help men harmonize their dreams and to direct their efforts to transcend the material conditions, the poverty and frustrations, the meanness and the pettiness and destructiveness of their own natures, and the evil in the world around them. It has helped them stand up as men in life and it has helped them face death.

MOVEMENT AWAY FROM
TRADITIONAL RELIGION

Although traditional myths are still believed and rituals are practiced by large sections of the population in almost every nation, increasing numbers of human beings are no longer able to accept the revelations of traditional religion as an authentic and binding faith to live by. People do not find them relevant or helpful. Promises of God's intervention in personal crises of sickness, hunger, unemployment, and poverty, or in family troubles, have not been fulfilled. A special providence intervening in natural law to protect a community or nation from plague and famine, earthquake and volcano and war, has been seen to be an illusion. Finally, belief in a special and exclusive relationship to a God in one religious group or nation or race as a "Chosen People" perpetuates illusions which still endanger the human world. The identity with an ancestry and a past is necessary. But as long as identity brings about extremes of group ego and beliefs in group superiority and God-given destiny to dominate others, it makes for division and hatred and violence. We see it widespread in wars between religious, racial, and national groups. Identity and group pride and solidarity can have positive value only if they afford such security to human beings that they can reach out beyond their ancestry and tradition to include the larger human community with trust and cooperation and sharing of life.

In a time of great insecurity and conflict and change, some people turn fervently to extreme doctrines of religious fundamentalism. Others embrace evangelical cults of sin, salvation, and the mystic unions with some larger cosmic force. But where do the unchurched go? They are many and increasing. They are people who know what they no longer believe. But is that enough? Can they, without religious affiliations or observances of traditional beliefs and forms, have a positive approach to life and a faith to live by?

John Lovejoy Elliott, an outstanding teacher and leader of Ethical Humanism and much loved by human beings of all classes and religious backgrounds, used to say, "I have known good people who believed in God. I have known good people who didn't believe in God. But I have never known good people who didn't believe in people." By "belief in people" he did not mean merely an attitude but a positive approach to human relations, a commitment to an ethical life, a readiness to try to work things out to the best of one's ability.

Many human beings who are no longer part of any traditional religious community may strive for a meaningful life through work and devotion to their families and the community. Some turn to careers of service. Others make their contributions to a better life in their avocational activities. There can be no one definition of "the good life" for all people. For some it means acceptance of and obedience to a particular moral code, one of conventional conformity. For others, it means a life guided by a conscious choice of values and priorities which include respect for every human being, a recognition of the interdependence of all life, and a treasuring of the relationships and interplay of differences which can enrich and enhance life, the life of all.

One summer I participated as a guest speaker in a graduate seminar on religion. When I had finished my presentation, a young woman said, "If I didn't believe in God and Jesus Christ as our Savior, and if I didn't believe in a Final Judgment and reward or punishment in an afterlife, I wouldn't see any purpose in trying to live a good life. I wouldn't see any meaning in life."

How to answer this challenge? I said, "I do not think the existence of God can be proved or disproved. But let us assume, for purposes of argument, that it could be proved that there is no God, no power or supernatural force outside of nature and outside of man, that will guarantee the victory of good over evil, of love over hate. Would this mean that there is no reason for being kind and compassionate? Would this mean that we would have no reason to work for a more just society or a more peaceful world? I say that there would be *more reason* to be kind and compassionate, *more reason* to try to bring about a just society and a peaceful world. It would be up to us. We would have to face the question: 'What do we want to make of our life?' "

This is what we mean by the philosophy of Humanism: that human beings should live with a maximum sense of responsibility for shaping their own lives individually and collectively. "The human being should stand on his own feet." He should do so with maximum self determination and sense of equality. He should do so without the illusion that he enjoys absolute security of survival or a guarantee that his values will be fulfilled by a divine power. If we wish to meet the challenge of fulfilling the distinctly human talents and human roles which are potential within the human being, we must cultivate greater ethical sensitivity and ethical judgment in relationships. And we must strive to create a more ethical culture, a civilization in which human beings can share freedom and use it for trust and cooperation and sharing life.

But whatever their concepts of a good life, and whether they are traditionally religious or nonreligious, human beings have deep needs at certain times of life. At such times they may go back to traditional religion for help, or they may work out their needs through secular substitutes—as when they go to the city clerk or a justice of the peace for a wedding. At the death of a loved one, they may decide to do without a funeral or memorial service, or they may ask a friend to say a word. But many of the nonreligious or "unchurched" call on the Ethical Culture Societies or the Humanist Fellowships for help.

Ideally, a ceremony should be an expression in which all those present participate. They may participate by presence and silence, but by active, not passive, presence and silence. For the important elements are the need and concern they feel, their expectations and readiness and openness to a shared experience of spiritual depth and dimension. In my experience, human beings in the crises of life are moved by awareness of the pain and suffering and waste of human life but also by a sense of life's possibilities and hopes and dreams. At such times people are more capable of responding to the deepest emotions and the highest aspirations of the human spirit. They tend to transcend self, and experience a feeling of being part of something greater than themselves. This is what makes the ceremonies of Humanism necessary and possible.

Just as there are ceremonies to celebrate the important events in the life of individuals and families, so there are community celebrations of shared values. The communal celebrations need not be concerned with supernatural myths or rituals; they are opportunities for bringing people together with a focus on ethical and human values—a joyous and courageous commitment to the quality of relationships and the development of human potentials. Among the ceremonies and celebrations which mark advances in the life of humankind are: The Festival of Light, Festival of the Children, and Festival of Bread and Peace. There are also many "happenings," celebrations and anniversaries which have to do with the gift of nature and the achievements of the human world—Celebrations of Music and *the* Arts, Festivals of Explorations and Inventions, Festivals of Freedom and Justice, the Commemorative Ceremonies of the lives of great individuals, and of great moments in history of the local and national communities.

The ceremonies of Humanism cannot be fixed and inflexible, repetitious and impersonal. Each is an expression which is shaped by the particular people concerned with the situation. Each is unique. Those of us who conduct such services do not speak with authority from on High. We speak out of the midst of the people, their need, their mood, and our sense of their ideals and aspirations.

In this book I share some of my experiences with the ceremonies of Humanism as I have known them. The calls for our services have come from individuals and families of all religious, racial, and national and class backgrounds.

A ceremony cannot make the sun rise or stop an earthquake, even if people believe it will. It cannot cause some power outside of man to intervene in the laws of nature on behalf of an individual or group or nation, a particular race or religious sect. It cannot assure favor to those who are more honest or just or loving than most. Nor can it save the human species if human beings persist in working destruction and death against each other and against life itself.

But a ceremony can bring people together. It can bring them together at an important time to share responsibility and make common commitment. It can celebrate the joyous and challenging situations of life. It can commemorate and keep alive the memory and influence of persons and achievements. The ceremonies of Humanism can meet needs and express potentialities that lie at the heart of human experience. They can enrich and bring meaning to the spiritual lives of mankind. They can help human beings continue the search for a faith to live by, a faith consistent with the best in human thought and feeling, a faith which will help the individual fulfil] his potentialities for a creative life. They can help humankind find ways of meeting the challenges of nature and the most difficult problems of the world of human relationships.

Without Burnt Offerings

NAMING

Introduction

If ever there is a time when we can say "yes" to life, it is at the birth of a child. The feeling of wonder and beauty is born and reborn again with each new life. It is indeed a time for celebration.

Among primitive people, and in the traditions of ancient civilizations, births and namings were occasions for ceremonies with prayers and gifts to supernatural powers to assure protection and support for the new life, and a naming ritual to mark the individual and his identity. Today, for those who believe in a divine supernatural power, it is still natural to acknowledge the gift of life with thanks and praise and gifts. In Christianity, the christening stresses identity with God, Jesus Christ, the Church, the Bible, and rites which wash away the taint of Original Sin and assure salvation and resurrection. In Judaism, the naming, and, in the case of male babies, the circumcision, is the occasion for re-establishing identity with the Old Testament and commitment to the teachings of the Commandments, the Laws of Moses, the authority of Yaweh, and the loyalty to Israel.

In our time, many traditionally religious people as well as Humanists and rationalists, tend to omit naming ceremonies for the newborn. No one questions the child's need for a name, the surname to mark the family association and the first name to mark and identify this individual as a particular person.

But why a ceremony? A name can be given by parents without a ceremony. The baby would not know the difference, but the cere-

1

mony could have an effect on the newborn's life in the years to come. Experience shows that a naming ceremony may meet human needs more important than the name itself and the act of naming. For the naming brings together those who are part of the newborn's ancestry and identity—the parents, grandparents, aunts and uncles, friends, fellow workers, and neighbors. In the midst of a diversified society and confusion of "who he is" and what he identifies with in religious beliefs and national and racial background, this is the group of human beings who will be the answer to his need for identity. Theise will be the stable, continuous members of the human community who care about him and can help him when he has need. He may be secure enough not to need an identity through ancestry. He may reject it or outgrow it, but it will be there if he ever needs it.

For those who are present at the ceremony there may be a number of different benefits. In many families the sons and daughters have moved away from their parents. With family dispersion, the members gather infrequently, usually only at the death of someone close. Where relationships are unified, friendly, and affectionate, the naming is a happy excuse for a reunion. Where the family is divided or alienated, the naming may be an occasion for communion and reconciliation. And where the newborn is the product of an inter-marriage, the naming is an opportunity for two sets of parents to reach out to one another with tolerance and understanding for the sake of their grandchild. It may help reconcile parents with the son or daughter who had married "out of the fold"; they may also at last accept the son-in-law or daughter-in-law whom they had rejected. For the naming ceremony can help bring about a miracle. It can do so because there is magic ia a newborn child. In part it is the dependence and the helplessness of the infant. In part it is the realization of the tremendous possibilities of growth and development, an awareness that this little being will become a man or woman, a human adult—and also that the baby is a product of the parents' own genes, their seed and blood. He will perpetuate something of themselves.

At the naming ceremony, the language must be simple and informal: words of welcome, wishes for the future, and the responsibility of all those present to protect and support and nourish this new life. As in other ceremonies of Humanism, the appeal is to human beings for a better life, not an invocation from on High but a call to the decent and just and loving element in human nature.

> Eyes are wonderful things to have.
> Everyone has two,
> Even a baby.
> Like stars they shine,
> Mirrors of the soul,
> Windows on the world.

Welcome

The room is full of you.
You are the newborn.

If you could always be
The child you are,
We'would gladly
Smash the watches and the clocks,
Tear up the calendars
To keep you young and free from care.

But you have a life to live,
So many discoveries,
The colors of earth,
The music,
Loving and being loved.

Your face will show what you are.
Your voice and smile and talents will identify you.
Most of all, your life
Will give your name meaning.

Now, John, will you name your son?

What's My Name?

*For the last fifteen years of her life, Eleanor Roosevelt
invited various groups of people to he her picnic
guests at Val Kill, her cottage near Hyde Park. For the
children of the Wiltwyck School for Boys, the picnic
was a special treat. Wiltwyck had heen created as a
residential center for hoys who were neglected or mis-
treated or had gotten into difficulties at home or in
school or in the streets. The grounds and facilities at
Val Kill were just right for a summer picnic. Besides,
the warmth and spirit of Eleanor Roosevelt made the
day one they never forgot. On one such picnic one little
boy seemed to feel the need for her attention and some
confirmation of his identity.*

A little boy runs up to the hostess.
"Mrs. Roosevelt," he says breathlessly,
"Do you remember me?"
She smiles. "Of course I do."
"What's my name?" he asks.
"I wish I could remember."
"Will you remember if I tell you my name?"
He tells her his name.
Then every half hour throughout the rest of the day
He returns again and again,

Always asking, "Mrs. Roosevelt, what's my name?
Do you remember me?
What's my name?
Mrs. Roosevelt, do you remember me?
What's my name?"

A Naming Where
There Is Another Child

Bobbie had been an only child for the first three years of his life. He was the darling of his parents and his grandparents. For some time he had been told there was going to be a little baby in the family. He had had to adjust to the fact that he couldn't play rough with his mother. He had had to face the fact that his mother had gone to the hospital. Preparations had been made for the new baby—room changes, shopping for a crib, the arrival of things for the baby. There were more phone calls and visits from his grandparents. His mother had come back from the hospital and had brought home his new baby sister. And now it was Sunday after- noon, the day for something called a naming ceremony. It was going to be a party with lots of people, and there were flowers and tables with all kinds of food and candies. His father had bought him a new suit and a new toy. He stood at the door, all dressed and hair brushed, ready to greet people as they arrived.

When his grandparents arrived, and his aunts and uncles and some neighbors and friends, he said, "Hello. Would you like to come and see my new toy?"

When it was time for the naming, the father brought a special chair, and the mother sat in it, holding the baby. The father took Bobbie by the hand. The father and Bobbie stood near me. The baby was no problem. She had been well fed and was pleasantly half-awake, but very ready to doze off. Bobbie, on the contrary, was restless and keyed up enough to warrant attention. It seemed to me that I would do better to address myself to him. I was sure those present would understand.

"Will you come and see my toy?" asked Bobbie.

"Yes, Bobbie, I'll come and see your toy, but not now. Later. I have a story to tell you. Some of us knew your mother and your father long ago when they were just friends. Then they loved each other and they decided to get married and find a home and live together. Did you know that?"

"Yes," said Bobbie.

"Then, when they found a lovely place to live, you were born. Some of us remember when you were a little baby. You know, when a baby is born it is naked and it has no clothes. It can't hold its head up and it can't feed itself or dress itself. It can't do anything. That's why your mother had to take care of you. And you didn't even have a name. So we had a naming ceremony, and all of us were at the party. And your mother held you just the way she is holding your baby sister now. And when your mother held you, I said to your father,

'Now give your son his name and call him by his name.' And you know what? Your father said, 'I name you Robert, or Bobbie.' And now you have another baby in the family."

"Yes," said Bobbie.

"Yes, it's your baby sister, and she has no name. So we're having a party for her. We are all glad that she was born into your family. We want to welcome her into your family. We want to say how glad we are that she is born into such a lovely home, with such a father and mother, and you for her brother. We are glad she was born into this country, where people, everybody, can be free. We want to wish that she will always be well and not be sick. We want her to be strong and bright so she will be fun to play with and will have fun out of her life. We think she will grow up to be a wonderful girl, and a friend of yours, and your sister."

Bobbie said, "You know what—"

"Now, I want to ask you a question. Please listen carefully. If you fell and were hurt, do you think we would help you? All of us? And if *we* were hurt and in trouble, would you help us if we called you? I think we would help you. I think you would help us. Now, suppose your sister fell and was hurt. Suppose she was lost. Wouldn't you help to find her? Would you help her if she needed you?"

"Yes, but—"

"Well, now your sister needs something. She needs it right now. Do you know what it is? She needs a name. Because when a person has a name, we know who he is. We know you are Bobbie. When we call your name, we know we are calling you. If your sister has a name, we can call her and talk to her and know her. So now I am asking your father to take your sister in his arms and give her her name and call her by name."

The father took his baby daughter in his arms and said, "Your mother and I have named you Deborah. We call you Debbie."

The mother called her daughter by name, "Deborah."

Bobbie put his hands out to me. "Deborah! And now will you come and see my toy?"

The Fatherless

Whatever qualms I may have had about performing a Naming Ceremony, they were set aside in 1943 when I received a call from an elderly black couple who lived in Harlem. Although they had been members of a Protestant church in their early years and had been married in it, they were now members of the Ethical Culture Society. Would I name the baby of a black girl who had become pregnant by a soldier? She had come from the South without any family and was living alone in Harlem. The couple had become aware of her situation, had taken care of her during her pregnancy, and had seen to it that she had proper hospital care. Now they were helping her in the first months of adjustment.

The girl was distressed. Brought up in the Baptist Church, she wanted the baby christened. But she had no husband or family. The couple suggested that she might have the equivalent of a religious ceremony with the naming done by a Leader of the Ethical Movement, without any theology. It could be in their home with just a few friends present and without embarrassment.

Since we had no fixed or prescribed rituals, I had to work out the form myself. To prepare for the occasion, I read the material of the religious ceremonies of Baptist and Methodist denominations. It seemed to me that the young mother and those who might be present would be just as satisfied and perhaps helped more if I tried to work out a naming ceremony which would be in keeping with their feelings and mine.

In the simple working-class living room decorated with flowers bought for the occasion,' the elderly couple and a few neighbors stood in a circle around the young mother with the infant in her arms. When the introductions and preliminary friendly exchanges were over, we shared a few moments of silence.

Even before I began to speak, I felt inadequate and troubled. Here I was, welcoming a child into the world, but was he really welcome? The pregnancy had not been wanted. There was no father, no marriage, no family or home. How could the young mother support him and care for him adequately? Was he not born into poverty? Was he not black in a predominantly white community, a white world which would see him through prejudiced eyes and deny him his rights and reject him with practices of discrimination and segregation? Where could he find a true welcome as a member of the human race? Where could he find a home with warmth and food and schooling and the opportunity to grow and fulfill his promise?

I could not ignore the reality. I had to find words that spoke truth, reality not glossed over with false poetic illusions. I fumbled for thought and word. What I said on that occasion was something like the following.

"Every child born into the world is precious. We who are gathered here in this place know that this child is especially precious to every one of us. It was said of old, 'There is a light that lighteth everyone that cometh into the world.'

"Some children are fortunate from birth. They are born to riches and family and home. They are completely accepted and wanted and loved. They can be sure of protection and care. We deem them fortunate.

"For others life is not always so easy. Their physical needs are not so easily met. There is no beautiful home to start with. A large family with all the good things of life may be lacking. But whatever the difficulties, there is a mother and there is a humanity we can draw upon. And the child has a strength and will to live. The little heart beats and the good warm blood moves through his body. His lungs draw' in the good air, he is fed and nourished, and he grows stronger. He reaches out his hands to touch and know the world. And nothing in the world will stop him from seeing and hearing and reaching out. The more he is loved, the more he becomes a person. And even if he suffers rejection by some, he finds strength and confidence and faith because others have faith in him. With our support he can overcome poverty and overcome rejection. He may even be a better and grander person because he learns how to overcome."

This was my welcome. Following this, I expressed the wishes we all had for him. Then followed the charge to those present to help assure the conditions and resources that would give this child a chance to live and fulfill his needs and his potentialities. The mother called the child by the name she had chosen. Then each person present in the room made a wish for the baby.

I thought then, and I think now more than ever, that every child should be born wanted, cared for, and loved. This is more possible where pregnancies are controlled and planned for, and where a stable man-and-woman love relationship is regularized by marriage. But there are unplanned births in families, in many instances without the love or means to care for a child and to nourish it. So also there are pregnancies where there is love but no planning or means of providing care. And there are instances where those drawn to one another provisionally and temporarily are not capable of being adequate parents. War and civil strife, poverty and racial fear and deprivation are not the best conditions for the birth and rearing of children. True, throughout history human beings have brought forth their young and reared them despite difficulty and danger and deprivation. And they have produced the kind of individuals who have character and talents and a capacity for humanity and love.

When a baby is born, what is the important question? Should we ask, "Was it born in wedlock?" Shall we ask its religion or race, whether it is black or white? The real question is: Does the human community take it as a member of the human race, as one of its own?

The important reality is the fact of a new life. This is legitimacy. There is no place in an enlightened community for the distinction between legitimate and illegitimate.

All children, whatever the circumstances of their birth, must start the race of life at the same starting point and run that race under the same rules. Only equality at the start can make a race fair and the winner a true winner. Whatever makes the race unfair must be done away with. All children are legitimate and must start even.

Cathy

As I was leaving my office at the end of the day, a young couple approached me. "Mr. Black, we have a problem we would like to discuss with you. Can you spare the time?" Their expressions were serious as I led them back into my office.

"We have been married for a little over a year," the young man said. "We now know that we made a mistake. We weren't really ready for marriage and we aren't really well mated or ready to make a life together. We've thought it out and talked it out at great length. The problem is that my wife is pregnant. The baby will be born five months from now. We want to give it away for adoption. But we want to be sure that it is given to a couple who have a happy marriage, a good home, who will take good care of the baby and love it as their own. We are both nontheists. We don't believe in the old religious teachings about God. We don't belong to any church. Can you find a couple who will be warm and loving—without theistic and sectarian religion? We've heard some of the Ethical Society broadcasts and read some of the literature. It's the way we look at life. That's why we came here for help."

"First, I wish I could be sure you really have to divorce each other," I answered. "Have you exhausted all the possibilities of working it out together? Have you really thought out what is best for the child?"

They took turns answering me. What they said was substantially the following: "We met at college. We were good students and had many interests in common. But we were too young. It didn't work. We care about each other, but we just aren't happy together. We know now that we can't make the kind of marriage we want. We've had counseling separately and together. It wouldn't be fair to us and it wouldn't be fair to the child. We want the child brought up in a happy family and in a home that can give it love."

"Assuming this is so, how do you know that you will be able to give up the baby after it's born? It isn't easy, you know. And once you give the baby to another family, you can't change your mind. It's final and permanent. You give up all right to the child. Won't you be torn apart emotionally when it comes time to part with the baby? You will never see the baby again, once it is born."

"I've been all through that with my therapist," said the young woman. "It took many sessions. You see, it's all settled in my mind, and the therapist agrees. I feel sure I can do it."

"It means that the adopting father and mother will come to the hospital with a nurse. They will take the baby home with them. You will not know who they are and you can never see or visit them or the child. Can you make peace with that?"

"We are sure of ourselves. It will be best for the child and best for us."

I said, "A number of couples with happy marriages and good homes and a love of children are eager to adopt children. I can think of one couple that might be just right to have your baby."

After an additional conference and their indication to me that they had a lawyer to represent them, I called the couple I had in mind. They came to see me. I gave them the information they requested and asked that they select a lawyer. During the next month the lawyers drew up the necessary papers and filed them. The adoption was approved by the Surrogate's Court.

Two months later, when the baby was born, the adopting mother and a nurse brought the baby home from the hospital. Approximately two months after that, the adopting couple asked for a naming ceremony.

When all the guests were gathered in the living room, the mother brought the baby. It is impossible to say how beautiful she was, and what she did to the people gathered there to see her and share in the celebration of her life. I spoke as follows.

"How shall we welcome you into the world? All our flowers and all our wine cannot express how happy we are at your birth. All the caresses of our eyes and hands cannot measure the fullness of our love. We cannot hold you close enough.

"We welcome you into the world of light and shade, of work and play, of laughter and tears, the evil and the good.

"We welcome you as one born of earth and yet more than earth, possessing the qualities and possibilities of the human.

"We welcome you into the human community, this nation, and the family of humankind. In you we have hope for a better life. In you we all share a new life, your inborn gifts and new ways of seeing. In your life our lives will be continued.

"May you have a healthy body with strength to stand against all that may threaten you, and may you have the courage and skill to do whatever is required of you and what you most desire to do. May you have a good intelligence, to learn what you need to know, and the power to pursue the truth you seek. May you be fearless and tender. May you enjoy the warm sun on your face and the flow of wind and water on your body. May you love the beauty of the world, its flowers and trees, the mountains and flowing streams, the movement of all living things. And may you know the music and the rhythm of nature and the drama and poetry of man's creations. Above all, may you know the comradeship of good friends and the meaning of generosity and compassion, the love of many and the love of one above all others.

"'And now we call upon your families and friends, to aid you and serve you. We are part of your personal world, responsible for guard-ing your freedom, your life, and your opportunities. Today we think of the other children who will share the life of your generation, whose welfare is inseparable from your own. May we all help make a more just and peaceful world for you and for all those whose lives are linked with yours."

Then, while the mother held the child, I turned to the father. "John, will you now name your daughter?"

And the father said, "We name you Cathy. We will treasure you as our daughter. We will love you and cherish you all the years of our lives. We hope you will always be happy with us and proud of your name. We call you Cathy because of a cherished and beloved friend. We know that the name will be a joy to all who know you."

I then read an ancient Irish pagan blessing which had been brought by one of the guests:

> May the blessing of light be with you always,
> Light without and light within.
> May the sun shine upon you and warm your, heart
> Until it glows like a great fire
> So that others may feel the warmth of it,
>
> And may the light of your eyes
> Shine like two candle lights
> In a window at night bidding the wanderer
> To come in out of the dark and the cold.

> And may the blessings of the rain be upon you,
> The sweet and tender rain,
> May it fall upon your spirit
> As when flowers spring up and fragrance fills the
> air.
>
> And may the blessings of the great rain
> Wash you clean and fair,
> And may the storms always leave you stronger
> And more beautiful.
>
> And when the rains are over
> May there be clear pools of water
> Made beautiful by the radiance of your light,
> As when a star shines beautiful in the night
> Pointing the way for all of us.

Ten years later I asked the adopting parents, "What does Cathy know and think about being adopted?"

The mother answered, "We told her she was adopted. We told her when she was so little that she probably didn't understand it at all. Later, when she was a bit older, she wanted to know.

"Cathy asked me, 'Where were you when I was born? What was I like when I was a baby?' And, I told her that we wanted a baby to be born to us. But when this didn't happen, we looked everywhere. 'We saw many children, but of all we saw, we chose you. We chose you because you were the child we wanted and loved.' She didn't know what it meant, but she talked about it to her friends in kindergarten and in the early grades. Pretty soon many of the children said they wished they had been adopted. And one day when she was a bit older, she said that when she grew up she would have one baby biologically and then she would adopt a lot of children."

A Child Adopted
by a Single Woman

Some men and women want children whether they are married or not. Today the single person can adopt a child if he or she truly loves children, is well-adjusted, and can provide a good home in which a child can grow.

In such cases a naming ceremony can fulfill a special need by making public the adoption of the child to family and friends. An adopting single mother who had worked for many years for child welfare and the rights of children called to ask if I would conduct a naming ceremony. For the occasion she invited her parents, who now had the joy of an additional grandchild. She invited her brothers and sisters, who were now the uncles and aunts, and her nieces and nephews, who were now the cousins of her child. In addition she brought together her friends and fellow workers, who had shared her work in education, social services, Family Court, and the study of conditions in institutions for children.

I arrived at the lovely apartment of the adopting mother to find an enthusiastic and exuberant party. A number of friends and fellow workers, as well as members of the family, had brought their children, who were having a good time, too. Two of the children of the family were to be the equivalent of godfather and godmother to their new cousin.

When I suggested that the naming begin, and when everyone had quieted down, the baby, who had appeared well fed and sleepy, suddenly came to life. Even in his mother's arms he became restless. Possibly because I was the only one speaking, he began to reach out to me. His mother passed the baby to me while I was trying to tell him what we meant by naming him. But in my arms he became even more restless, so I passed him back to his mother. I rejoiced in his aliveness and his vitality, but it did make it difficult for me to concentrate when I spoke as follows.

"Every human life is precious and every baby born is precious. Some are born to us and some are given to us, and that is a very special relationship.

'We have come together now to make this a golden day for all of us, for the family and friends, and above all the mother.

'The way we look at you and the way we caress you is a very inadequate expression of the love that we feel for you.

"We hope you will always stand firm and walk secure with the warmth of the earth in your body and the fire of the sun in your spirit. We wish for you the strength of the rocks and mountains, the gentleness of grass and flowers with all their colors and fragrance. May you feel the joy of the wind as it moves through the fields of grain and tosses the branches of the trees of the forest.

"We invite you to know the waters of the earth, the springs and brooks and rivers as they flow to the sea. May you know the rhythm of the waves and moving tides and the wild storms, the joys of cleansing and life-giving waters, and the quiet of the ponds and lakes.

"May you always stand on your own feet and walk your own paths with faith in yourself. And may you know what it means to love and be loved. May you always be glad that you were born. May you always have a zest for life. And may you learn and grow in your sense of what it means to be human.

"The *name* we give you is only one way to know you. We hope that your name will mean joy to yourself and others. We will always know you by your face, your smile, the things you said before you knew words. We will love you for the new life you bring to your mother and the family and to the enrichment of life for all of us. Above all, we will love you for yourself."

Holding her baby son in her arms, the adopting mother said, "For me, and I hope for all my family and friends, this is a moment of great joy. I am fortunate to have found a son. He is a gift of the gods, as the Greeks would have said long ago. I name him Theodore. It comes from two Greek words: *theos,* meaning God, and *dor on,* meaning gift. May he always be bright with the warmth of the sun,, and may the light of his spirit shed friendship and love wherever his life takes him."

I added a wish: "We know that your son will grow under your devoted and loving care. For Theodore I use the words of Virgil: 'May your name endure with honor as long as the rivers run to the sea, as long as the sun casts the shadow of the mountains over the slopes and heaven shows the fire of the stars.' "

The Adopting Single Mother

Not flesh of my flesh,
Not bone of my bone,
But still miraculously my own,
Never forget, even for a minute:
You weren't born under
my heart
But in it.

—Source unknown

Where In-Laws Are United

I have said that there is a magic in a baby that can work a miracle when nothing else can. When I say "miracle," I do not mean supernatural or mystic powers. Nor do I refer to gushy sentimentality. I mean that the newborn baby has a sort of magnetic force which brings out the sensitive and sympathetic and generous concern of people. It evokes an impulse which is outgoing rather than ego-centered and makes people ready to identify and give to, rather than take from, life. I do not mean to attribute more magic and magnetic power than there is. It is not unlimited. But it can have strength at a crucial time.

On a Sunday afternoon I was driven out to the home of a man and woman whom I had married two years before in New York. They had asked me to name their baby. My driver was the woman's brother. On the way out to the suburbs in New Jersey, he indicated that his parents had never been reconciled to the marriage of his sister. They were devout members of a conservative Protestant church, and they had opposed her marriage to a Jew. In fact, the father had not attended the wedding. I asked the brother how he felt about it. He shrugged. "I wouldn't have married a Jew. But if she wanted to, she should have the right."

"Will your parents be at the naming?" I asked.

"Yes," he said, "I think my dad has come around—not all the way, but he can't stay away from this. My mother won't permit him to stay away. Besides, he may be curious."

I remember thinking that I had seen some reconciliations at death—a father and son in a hospital where a wife and mother lay dying, and two brothers who hadn't spoken to one another for years, reconciled and embracing at their father's grave. As at death, so now with birth, maybe a new life could begin for older people too.

The house in the suburbs was attractive and equipped with all the middle-class comforts; everything was in good taste, but, most of all, it had the atmosphere of a real home where everything had been chosen out of a desire for informality and flexibility and warmth for family living.

After being greeted by the new father, I met the two sets of grandparents and congratulated them. Friends and neighbors were arriving. The husband led me upstairs to see his wife and their baby. We talked about how we would have the ceremony: we would all stand, the mother would bring in the baby and hold him while I spoke; then the father would call the name of the child and say whatever he had prepared; finally the father would take him in his arms and pass him to each of the grandparents, beginning with the maternal grandfather.

Downstairs the atmosphere in the living room was politely friendly in a way that might have been prescribed in a book of etiquette. Conversation was restrained. But when the young mother came in with the baby in her arms, it was as if someone had turned up the lights. The afternoon sun through the lace curtains wasn't really any stronger than before, but there was more warmth and light, and something changed the tight and solemn atmosphere. After I had spoken, the father called the child by name. The baby was taken into the arms of one grandparent after another. A neighbor held up a glass of wine and proposed a toast to the child and parents and grandparents. I returned to the city with no question in my mind that a ceremony can have meaning and value.

INITIATION

Introduction

In every human society the transition from childhood to adulthood is marked by some ceremonial recognition of the change of status and function and responsibility of the individual.

In a primitive or preliterate society, initiation of the young into adulthood is relatively simple. The community is likely to be small and homogeneous, with a common history and tradition. Social customs are static, and without a written language there is no vast accumulation of learning. The young, as hunters, fishermen, warriors, and homemakers, are trained by their elders and, when they reach physical and sexual maturity, are initiated in ceremonies which enable them to marry and participate in the life and councils of the community.

Today, in modern society, initiation of the boy and girl into adult life is far more complicated. Society is vast, heterogeneous, a network of interdependent groups with many different backgrounds, traditions, and outlooks, the products of religious, racial, national, and class differences. In our age of technology the young have to learn to deal with motor cars and trains and planes, machines and electronic devices, typewriters, television sets, computers, and mass-production assembly lines. They face high concentrations of population, high mobility, and relationships on regional, national, and global levels. All this they have to know and understand in a time when customs, laws, and institutions are undergoing drastic and rapid change in the midst of a high degree of human differences and human conflict.

It has been generally assumed that the preparation of the young for life in industrial and urban society is the responsibility of the schools. But the initiation of the young requires more than schooling, more than knowledge and skills. If some of the simpler so-called primitive cultures had a series of initiations to bring youth into full participation in the adult community, how much truer is it that our youth have to go through a series of involvements, each of which ends one phase of life and begins another. The initiation has to be in the experience, in the living. The first is our entrance as infants into the family of our birth and our adjustment to family relationships. The second is our admission to the schools and the educational process. Third is our movement into, employment, the production of goods or services, and our involvement in work relationships. A fourth phase is love and marriage and the creation of home and family. Through these stages in a democratic society the individual becomes increasingly a participating member of the larger community, sharing power and responsibility to shape the common life. These successive involvements in ever-deepening and broadening relationships are the true preparation and initiation into the life of society and the world.

Whatever our attitudes may be, the process of preparation and involvement is not simple or certain. Where the family has been authoritarian and rigid, overdemanding and overprotective and too turned in on itself, the child has been inhibited from growing and connecting with the life of the school and community. Where school has been narrowly academic and unresponsive to the changing world, the students have lost motivation for learning, have dropped out, and have revolted against the educational institutions which were most charged with their preparation for life. The identity crisis and the alienation of youth in the contemporary scene is understandable not only because of the family and school, but also because of the experience of youth in the day-to-day life of the streets and the relationships and values of the community and the nation. On every hand youth sees the contradictions and violations of the ideals taught in the name of democracy and religion. The conditions which foster inequality and injustice, widespread deprivation and frustration, hostility and violence, account for some of the disillusionment and cynicism. Deeper than these are the individualistic and materialistic values which breed insecurity and greed, exploitation and corruption. For sensitive and intelligent youth who have a decent sense of values, who have a social concern about people, the question may well be, who is initiating whom? And for what, for what quality of life?

There can be no one single ceremony of initiation. It takes more than achieving physiological puberty to make a boy into a man or a girl into a woman. Initiation requires mental and emotional adulthood, social and ethical maturity. Initiation may take all the years of a lifetime.

In these circumstances an initiation ceremony can be an empty formality or, even worse, a pious verbalization of democratic ideals or religious beliefs or patriotic sentiments. I hope the selections which follow are free from such weaknesses. For in the present mood of our society it is important to try to keep faith with youth for the long run beyond the present phase of confusion and turmoil. I hope I have expressed with a minimum of formality a maximum of sincere provocation for growth and clarification of the values worth living for.

The Story-Teller
—The Listeners

The use of the story as an instrument to focus thought and evoke emotional response is very old among the teachers of the past. As an Ethics teacher for many years, I have told stories to classes and to school assemblies. In a particular morning assembly I had the feeling that the children had identified so much with the boy I was talking about, that they were living his experience and had taken the story for their own.

Looking into their upturned faces,
The words flowed out of my mouth
With the story of a lonely hungry child.
Then I began to feel

The story alive with its own movement;
The children's eyes were shining,
They were alive,
I was left behind.
At the end they were applauding
Their own creation,
They were applauding life
And themselves.

"To Be Alive"

This is an excerpt from an address to children on completion of the Religious Education Program at the Ethical Culture Society.

Why do we have a ceremony to celebrate your graduation? We want everybody to know that you have passed—your parents and family and friends and everybody. We are proud of you. You should be proud too. But it's more than that.

I want to tell you about a particular person I saw years ago. A very beautiful woman. She was beautiful in her face, her eyes, her body, her arms and hands, her legs and feet—just about perfect. One thing was wrong with her. You could see right through her. She was made of glass.

Next to her were some buttons. If you pushed one button, her kidney lit up. If you pushed another button her liver lit up, and with another, her stomach. And every part lit up with a different color. Her lungs were blue. Her brain lit up purple, and all the nerves too, from the top of her head to the tips of her fingers and toes. And her heart lit up red right down through the arteries and the veins, even though she had no blood.

Something was missing. She stood still but she couldn't move. She had hands but she couldn't touch anything. She had ears but she couldn't hear, and eyes but she couldn't see. She had a brain but she couldn't think or know anything. She had no mind at all. And she had a heart but no feelings. She couldn't get angry or jealous. She couldn't be afraid or brave. And she couldn't hate or love anybody. You couldn't possibly imagine kissing her or marrying her. She was smooth and cold. She had no pulse or heart beating like yours and mine. She had no thermostat inside, no steady temperature of her own. She was as cold or as hot as the room. And if you hit her she would shatter into a thousand little pieces of glass.

Why do I speak of a glass woman? Because she had everything but one thing: she was not real. She was not alive.

You are alive! You are real! You think! You feel! You do know the value of things—what is true and false, beautiful and ugly, good and bad! But the glass woman had no sense of these things. She just stood there. She was dead.

Whatever else you may believe in life, you have to believe that you are real, that you are alive and becoming more alive. Your family and your school, every experience you have had should help you know what it means to be alive. You can find your way. You can decide what you want to be, you can say what you want to do with your life. You do not depend on the temperature of the room for your temperature. And you are not blown this way and that by the wind—you stand where you want to stand and move where you want to move. What you do does not depend on what people think but on what you think. You are able to say, "I have my own pulse. I have my own heart. I have my own thermostat. I have my own mind. I will choose whether to live or die. And I will choose what I will live for and what I will do with my life." Is this not the purpose of your growing, of your education? Isn't this what it means to be alive—and free?

Sixth-Grade Graduation

June 1972. Parents and grandparents, aunts and uncles, and faculty gathered in the Meeting House. With processional music, the double doors from the school opened. Framed in the light of the doorway, the first sixth-grader stood still for a moment, facing the assemblage, then walked slowly up the aisle to his seat. Each pupil followed in turn, pausing in the doorway to face the gathering, then walked in his own style, solemn or sprightly or with a comic expression; most of the girls in white and some of the boys in dark

suits, no two alike, each with a bit of color and some
special touch. When all were at their seats, one of the
students welcomed everyone to the final program of
their careers at the Ethical Culture Elementary School.
The class and faculty sang the school song. Then every
student participated in the music program that
followed, either by playing in the orchestra or in a
recorder ensemble or by singing in the class chorus.
Each part of the program was introduced by a student
of the graduating class. Finally, before they received
their diplomas, I was introduced and spoke.

Members of the Class of 1972, you look beautiful to me and you did the music program beautifully. But I wonder whether you are really ready for graduation. Perhaps there are still some things that should be tested before you get the diploma. Perhaps we should consider this assembly the last class. With this in mind, I put to you some propositions to think about.

Once upon a time a teacher thought that he should teach equality. This was in a country where the king had absolute power. The teacher went among the poorest people. His meetings with the farmers and peasants were held at night in their huts. In one hut the peasants were crowded together around a table. The only lamp lit their faces browned by the sun and wrinkled by years of hard labor in the fields. The teacher took out a bag of beans. He put one bean in the center of the table and said "That's the king." Then he made a circle of beans around it and said, "That's the royal family." Then he made another circle of beans and said, "That's the big landowners." Then he made another larger circle of beans and said, "That's the army." Then he put all the rest of the beans around the outside of the largest circle and said, "That's the people, that's you!"

"Now," he said, "where's the king?" One of the peasants stroked his beard and very slowly with his finger pointed to the bean in the center and said, "That's the king." "Right!" said the teacher.

Then the teacher said, "Where's the royal family?" Another peasant stroked his beard. Then he slowly pointed to the first circle of beans and said, "That's the royal family." "Right!" said the teacher.

Then the teacher said, "Where are the large landowners?" And one of the peasants stroked his beard and pointed to the second circle. "Right!" said the teacher.

Then the teacher said, "Where is the army?" Another peasant then pointed to the largest circle of beans.

"Now," said the teacher, "where are the people?" And another peasant pointed to the beans all around the table. "Right," said the teacher. Then he scrambled all *the* beans together and said, "Where's the king?"

Is that a good way to teach equality to the people? I'm not asking you to answer today, I'm just asking you to think about it. That's my first lesson in this last class.

There was a workman in a factory. It was his job to make bearings for cars. He could have been making parts for other things— radios, typewriters, or tractors. He followed the measurements on his blueprint and used his lathe with such care and accuracy that the bearings he made could replace each other. They were accurate to the thousandth of an inch.

There was a gardener. His job was to grow things. Were they all alike? He had to know the seed—whether it was corn or tomatoes or another vegetable, and the exact variety. But he had to know a lot more. He had to know the conditions under which things grow. He had to know the kind of earth and the fertilizer, and the right time to put the seed into the ground; if there was water enough; how to fight off the pests. His work was different from that of the man who makes things in the factory exactly alike. The gardener didn't make anything. He just had to know the conditions that would help things grow. He trusted in the forces of nature and worked with them.

Now there was a teacher. Was he like the factory worker who made products exactly alike to the thousandth of an inch? Or was he more like the gardener who had to know the conditions under which things grow? Suppose the teacher had twenty of you in a class. Would he or she make each of you exactly alike? Would he or she shape you or produce you? Or would he or she show respect for what you had in you, the seed of each of you? To try to find the conditions under which each of you would grow? And would you all grow exactly alike, or would each of you be different? The teacher is dealing with an organism, an individual, with intelligence and feelings. Each person is different. An individual has cells. Each of his millions of cells is his own, and they are arranged in him a little bit differently from the way they are arranged in any other individual.

The teacher has to respect that in deciding about the conditions for growth and learning. He has to know the needs of the child; the desires of the child, what is in a child's mind, what it feels, what it wants to be, what it wants to do.

When you get the diploma, it means that you have learned to learn. In fact, if it is a good school, it means that you have learned to teach yourself. You have become your own teacher. If the teachers are good, they don't really teach you very much. Yes, some facts and knowledge. Yes, some skills—how to shoot a basket, how to bake a cake, how to solve problems with the multiplication tables, how to write a sentence. The "know-hows." But, most of all, the teachers helped you to learn for yourself according to your own needs and desires. That's the real meaning of your diploma.

And the most important thing to learn is not about things and numbers and ideas, but about people. Your diploma is a sign that you can do things for yourself and for others and the community of which you are a part. You can put your education to use. If you keep on learning, you can put it to very good use. For the diploma is a sign that you are ready for something much bigger than you ever dreamed of. The human race has suffered from wars all through history. People who haven't even known each other have killed whole families and destroyed whole communities. We still have war. And within each nation and here in our country we have crime and violence. What are the causes of the conflict between people, the fears and hates? Many people need to work and want to work, but they are unemployed. Many people all over the world need food and shelter. They want good schools for their children. They want their families to enjoy the good things of life, but they lack the means. We hope your schooling will help you to deal with these problems.

The boys and girls of your generation will be your fellow citizens and neighbors in the years to come. They will share your life, in peace or war, in justice or crime and violence, in prosperity shared or extremes of rich and poor. Your life will be good or bad, depending on whether you respect one another and help one another and share life with one another. This too is the meaning of your diploma.

Through the years you have been here, you have walked through the halls and run up and down the stairs. You have used the rooms, the gym, the library. Your shoes have worn down the floors and the stairs. But this building was very well built. The foundations are solid; the walls are thick and strong. Next year in the fall, new classes will begin to use the school again. They too will wear down the floors and the stairs, and maybe they will put marks on the walls. But the building is strong; it will stand. It will be cleaned and used again and again for generations. We hope you will always be loyal to the school and support it. Stay well! Grow strong! And take care of yourselves.

The Assassination of President Kennedy

After President John Kennedy was shot on Friday, November 22, 1963, the principal and faculty of the Midtown Ethical Culture School arranged for a special assembly for children of the third through sixth grades. It was to he held the first period on Monday morning, before the children went to their regular classes. I was invited to speak.

Last Friday afternoon something happened in our country which doesn't happen very often. It was a very sad thing—but, if we think about it, we may learn something from it, and maybe it will not happen again.

If you live in the jungle you are not very safe. There are all kinds of wild animals, lions and leopards, snakes and alligators—all sorts of dangers. Not even an animal is safe in the jungle.

Let me tell you a story to show you what I mean and what it has to do with the death of our President. It's by a man who lives in the forest a great deal and -knows more about it than all of us put together. He is a scientist who knows nature. He knows the trees, flowers, birds and insects and animals.

His story goes like this: I was walking through the forest, and the sun was coming through the trees. The air was fragrant. It was cool in the shade. It was like a big cathedral, the tree trunks reaching upward, straight into the sky, and the branches arching out with the sun coming through. All of a sudden I heard birds crying. Then I saw a mother and a father bird hovering around a nest and crying and fluttering their wings. A raven was coming to attack their nest, their nestlings. And the mother and father birds couldn't do a thing about it. The raven went into the nest and he killed the little birds. Then he sat there, very proud of what he had done, with the sun shining on his sleek black coat of feathers. When this happened, all the birds in the forest began a kind of wailing, a cry, a sing-song of sorrow. The raven paid no attention. When he pleased, he flew away and left an empty nest behind him.

Then, as if by magic, the wailing stopped. There was a hush, a silence. At that moment a little song sparrow took heart and began to sing a different song. From his throat came a lively and a happy note. It passed from one bird to another on and on until all the birds were singing and the forest resounded with their song of joy, their song of life. It was as if they understood that a bad thing had happened. But the sad thing was over. It was time now to think not of death, but of life*

When I think of the President's death, I ask myself the question: Do we want to make a world where the human thing, the good in people, will conquer the jungle? For this is what President Kennedy

* Adapted from Loren Eisely's *The Immense Journey,* Random House, 1957.

stood for—that the weak should be safe, that we could all walk the earth without being afraid.

Now, sometimes a school trains you to sharpen your teeth and sharpen your claws so you can go out and get whatever you want for yourself. You have the attitude, "I am number one! Everything is for me! I am going to take what I can, no matter what I do to other people!" Sometimes a family does this. It can narrow a person so he cares only about the people who are like him, or who think the way he does. A person can grow up narrow in his mind and say, "My people are better than all other people. All the rest do not matter."

If a boy comes of a poor family, he may have a hard time getting an education and winning his way. If a boy has a rich father, sometimes he has a hard time just because his father is rich. Most of the people are not rich. They may say, "Why should we vote for a rich man's son? How can we be sure that he will be interested in our troubles and our hopes?"

John Kennedy was Catholic. You know that we had never had a Catholic as President. Many people have prejudices against people because of religion. Many people said, "He'll never be elected President." But many other Americans said, "Let's have an open mind. After all, a man's religion is his own business. Let's look him over and see what he is before we decide."

John F. Kennedy thought that the more you try to understand people who are different from you, of different colors, with different eyes, different languages, different history, the bigger you become in your mind and your heart. So, though he was very young when he was killed, our youngest President had become very wise. He had learned a lot in a short time about himself and about other people.

Many people in this country are saying, "This President was not shot just by one man who was crazy or full of hate; he was killed by all the people who hate, who permit a climate of violence." If the air gets too full of prejudice, pretty soon you are poisoned by it. If the water you drink gets too full of bad things, pretty soon you are poisoned by it. Maybe we have let the air get too full of people breaking the law, people driving faster than the speed limit, people pushing other people out of the way, the strong taking advantage of the weak, people expressing hate.

When I heard of President Kennedy's death on the radio, I thought not only of how shameful and unbelievable it was—but right away I wondered: Are we going to have disorder? Will we fall apart? Then I remembered that ours is a democratic government. It does not depend on one person, a king or anyone else. Our government was built by the people. And a long time ago, the people who wrote the Constitution knew that a President could be assassinated, and they provided for it.

You saw what happened. As soon as President Kennedy was killed, the Vice-President became the President. Just as, in battle, if a general is killed or a captain is wounded, immediately another officer takes his place. On a ship, if the captain is injured, the first mate takes charge. So our Vice-President took the oath and moved into the White House.

The wonderful thing is that everybody kept his head: the people in government, the Army, firemen, businessmen, all the teachers, doctors, lawyers—everybody stayed on his job.

When President Kennedy took the oath of office, he spoke of the relationships between countries, and he said, "Let's never be afraid to talk together, and let's never talk together because we are afraid. We should be able to talk together about the things that unite us. They are far greater and more important than the things that divide us.

He also said, and this he is saying to you, as if he were speaking to you, "Together let us explore the stars, conquer the desert, eradicate disease, explore the ocean depths, encourage art, music, literature, drama, all the beautiful things of life and commerce, and let both sides unite in all corners of the earth to heed the command of Isaiah, the great prophet of Israel, to 'beat our swords into plowshares and to free those who are oppressed.' "

If you have courage, you can do things. But if you live timidly and anxiously and do not overcome your fear, you cannot do anything! If you are afraid, you will never cross the street. You will never take a train or a plane. You will never go away from home to a party, or to college, or take a new job, or get married. You will just be afraid to live.

I hope you will never forget that when you were in school theie came a weekend in November 1963 when you and your family and the whole nation mourned the death of a young man who carried in his heart and in his mind a great understanding of the needs and the hopes of people. I hope that from his death and from his life, all of us will live with courage—so that we can help this nation fulfill the hope of freedom and equality and peace for all mankind.

Your Life and Your Faith

I gave this talk at a "Recognition Assembly," when teenagers completed the Religious Education Program of the Ethical Culture Society, May 1968.

Each of us has one life to live. We have a certain number of years. No one knows how long he will live. But our fear is not of death. Our fear is that we will not use our years well or get Your Life and Your Faith the most out of them. It would be a terrible thing to have wasted the years of one's life. The evil of the world is not just the hurt human beings inflict on one another; it is the waste of life. So many people never really find the way to live their lives in health and happiness, in productivity and love. Your life and mine are lived as we use the time to grow and fulfill our potentialities.

I hope we will all stand for freedom of the human spirit, freedom of the human mind and heart. Freedom is a means to an end. If we cannot find out how to use the freedom, what good is it? For when we speak of caring about freedom, we also have to mean responsibility for the ways we use freedom and what we use it for. At some point we have to decide what values will give the most meaning and purpose to our lives. What are the values we put first, and for which we would be willing to work and make sacrifices? Only if we are disciplined by our own sense of purpose can we make our choices and decisions as builders of families, working as productive and creative human beings and participating as citizens in a society where government is of the people, by the people, and for the people.

When we start to think of a life purpose, we can think of the world the way it is and of ourselves the way we are. We can also think of the world the way it might be and the kind of persons we might be. Hope is something beyond knowledge. Some things we know. Some things we hope for. When we believe in something which we do not know, hope for but cannot prove, then we have faith. We do not say that the things we value as good will positively come to pass. We hope so. And when we believe in our hope, we may stake our life on the possibility that our effort will make a difference. It is our faith that we can make a better world for all men and that we can become better people.

There is a hunger in people for more truth and more beauty and more goodness than the world has yet known. And we believe that it is in the relations of people with one another that human beings work out the most sacred things in life. Where relationships are unsound and unfair, where people neglect, deprive, mistreat, exploit, and reject others, there is bound to be insecurity, distrust, fear and hate. This means mental illness and emotional disturbance. It makes good family life, creative work, and a just society difficult. It makes peace within and between nations impossible. The more ethical the life we achieve, the more healthy and productive and happy we can all be. To strive for decency, fair play for everyone, and to fight for the rights of others as for our own—this is an essential need today. It is part of the struggle to fulfill the human quality in the human individual and in human society. If there is a purpose in the universe and in the evolution of the human species, we must try to find out what we mean by being true to ourselves, to our *human* nature. To commit ourselves to such a purpose is the heart of what we mean by religion. It is a true expression of appreciation for the gift of life and a true sense of reverence for life and commitment to fulfilling life.

An ancient philosopher said: "Because we know death we have to have the courage to live." Another ancient philosopher said: "Even though I must die, I need not whine about it. Even though I am imprisoned, I can still smile about it. Even though you chain my leg, you cannot chain my mind or my will or my spirit."

This is the undying spirit of man. We believe that it is a spirit which means freedom, but slso 2. spirit in which men hind, them‑ selves to their own highest purposes. It calls for intelligence and a good heart and courage.

On Being a Good American

Long before the current interest in pollution, waste, and ecology, Robert Marshall, graduate of the Ethical Culture Schools and friend, developed a passion for the out-of-doors, a respect for the beauty of nature, and a commitment to conserve our natural resources for all Americans. A few years after his death, 1 spoke of his life and work at a high-school convocation to celebrate Washington's and Lincoln's birthdays.

I want to tell a story about a boy I went to school with. He was the shyest and quietest boy in the class, and the shyest and quietest person I ever met. If you didn't know him, you might think he wasn't very smart. You might think he was dumb and couldn't speak. He had good ears to hear with, and clear eyes to see with, but he didn't speak unless he had to. He had a wonderful shy smile, and a wry sense of humor. He was a good athlete, excellent as guard in basketball and a dependable outfielder in baseball. Most of all, he was a good sport.

He loved to camp in the woods and to climb the mountains up in the Adirondacks. Sometimes he went with other boys and sometimes alone. He climbed every major peak in the Adirondack Range in New York State—many of the lesser mountains, and all forty-six that are over four thousand feet, like Whiteface, MacIntyre, and Marcy. He loved to sleep in the lean-tos, or out in the open, and to swim in the ice-cold mountain streams. Early one morning I was asleep in one of the lean-tos in the "Flowered Lands," curled up in my blanket, when I heard a crackling sound. I sat up and looked around. There was this young man cooking his breakfast over a campfire. I recognized Bob and asked when he had arrived. He answered, "I just got here about sunup, an hour ago. I came up over three peaks to get here."

When he graduated from high school, he wanted to be a forester. He didn't expect to make money; he wanted to protect the forests.

He loved the quiet of the woods. He knew how valuable the trees are to the future of this country. He wanted to live and work among them. He had paddled a canoe on the Saranac River and some of the lakes up in the mountains, and had seen what the fires had done where people had been careless and whole square miles of forest had been burned. All that you could see in some places now was the burned stumps of trees. And he saw where the lumber companies had cut trees down without planting young trees.

For years he walked the trails and climbed the fire towers, spotting and fighting fires. Then he asked for permission to make a special study. On the side of a big mountain range he set out gauges to measure the amount of water flowing off the mountainsides each day, each week, and each month of the year. He measured the water run-off on the side of the mountain both where the trees of the forest had been cut down and where the trees were still growing. He wanted to see whether cutting the trees made a difference in the amount of water that came down from the mountains. In his careful study, he found that in the springtime the snow melted faster on the land where the trees had been cut. The gauges showed that the water running off the land without trees filled and overflowed the streams down the mountain and flooded the land in the valley. Where the trees were still standing, the snow was protected from the sun by the shade of the trees and melted slowly into the earth. The trees had dropped so many leaves that they acted like a sponge, and they held the water. On the land where the trees still stood there were no spring floods. The water flowed slowly down the mountainside through all the months of the year. He also found that on the land without trees there were no roots or spongelike leaves or forest floor to hold the earth. So the flowing water washed away the precious earth, while the land that had the trees held the earth, and there was very little soil erosion.

With his kind of mind and restless spirit, Bob Marshall could not just accept the forest fires and floods without doing something about them. He decided that he needed facts. He set up more research studies and made his findings public to the lumber companies, the government, and the people. His reports, published in pamphlets and books, showed that the forests owned by the government were better managed, had fewer fires and better lumbering and reforestation policies than those owned and managed by private companies. He made recommendations showing how government could do a better job to help protect the forests owned by private companies.

He was so much respected for his work that he was made the Chief of the Division of Recreation and Lands of the U.S. Forest Service and Chief for the forests on Indian reservations for the Bureau of Indian Affairs. He visited the reservations to help the Indian tribes develop their forests and keep them free from fires and bad lumbering. He saw to it that they planted young trees when they cut old trees down. He helped more than one tribe to establish their own lumber mills and their own factories to make wood products.

He was co-founder of the Wilderness Society. He had the idea that in some places the land of this country should be kept as a wilderness, just the way it had been before the white man came. The

Indians had respected the land and all things that grow. They did not destroy the forests. They did not pollute the streams. He wanted large areas set aside that would not be spoiled by highways and hot-dog signs. He wanted wilderness areas set aside where animals and trees would be safe, and where people could enjoy unspoiled nature. If anybody wanted to go into a wilderness area he would have to walk in on his own feet or ride in on a horse. No cars would be allowed.

In his travels through the country, even when he held high positions in the government service, he often walked and rode on a horse, or paddled a canoe. This man who had been shy and quiet in school learned to speak with all kinds of people. He learned Indian languages. He studied and lived with Indians and Eskimos in Alaska, too. He was particularly interested in people who lived close to the earth and the mountains and the wilderness, places where the character of people could be known by what they were and what they did, rather than by the property they owned or the money they spent.

He worked so hard that he must have strained his heart. When he died, aged thirty-nine, people all over the country said, "We have lost a great American." He never waved the American flag. He never pretended to be a great patriot; he never talked about loyalty. But he surely lived loyalty. If you climb in the Adirondacks someday, you will come to a trail called the "Marshall Trail." And someday, if you visit Montana, you will come to a place called the "Robert Marshall Wilderness," the first tract of American land set aside by the government and the people in memory of a man who cared about the land

and the forests of this country, and the people of America.

He never spent much money on himself; he always lived very simply. In his will, he left his savings to be used to help the conservation movement, long before people began to talk about pollution and waste and ecology.

I speak of him this morning to you, the future citizens of this country. May you in your own way find work to do that will conserve what is good in the land and resources, and what will benefit the people who wish to live in freedom and share our rich heritage.

Martin Luther King Anniversary

It was a graduation ceremony of the Religious Education Program of the Ethical Culture Society and the anniversary of Martin Luther King's death. The program was planned by teenagers.

A student read from the Declaration of Independence:

We hold these truths to be self-evident, that all men are created equal. That they are endowed by their Creator with certain inalienable rights, that among these are Life, Liberty, and the Pursuit of Happiness. . . .

Another student spoke: "Our group has chosen this topic because in the years in which we have attended the school, violence has been a major occurrence in the world. As students, we feel it to be our responsibility to deal with this important aspect of our lives. The great revolutions, the American, French, and Russian, developed out of the root problem of a large segment of the population being ignored by the people in power. Paul Goodman, in *The New York Times* of April 28, 1968, writes, 'In this process, those who are disregarded as not quite persons, who are treated brutally and who fear not unjustifiably that they may be simply exterminated, desperately lash out with fire and riots, destruction and self-destruction.'

"But it is hard for us to imagine why anyone would want to destroy their own community. Psychiatrists tell us that feelings of self-respect and self-worth must be carefully nurtured by acceptance and love. Since we are young and still have lots of time, we must decide now: Do we want to find our country in ruins? I can only conclude and hope with Aesop, who tells us about a lion and a goat who are quarreling at a waterhole as to which should drink first. There was plenty of room for them to drink together, but nonetheless they quarreled, and were preparing to fight it out when they saw vultures wheeling low above them waiting for the battle and its aftermath. They decided to drink together."

A girl related her experiences as a white person living in Harlem with her family: "It has been seven years since my family and I moved to Harlem. I've been through some experiences which I think have changed me and given me the basis for my views on certain subjects in the world now. People say when you are young your character develops in relation to your environment and experiences. I feel that I have been greatly influenced by my experiences both within and outside of my home.

"In seventh and eighth grades no one was really interested in world affairs so much that they would discuss their own feelings with others. This year has been different. There were many things happening in the world that directly affected our generation. When Martin Luther King was assassinated we realized that not only had a man been killed, but a man who had had great dreams and hopes for the Negro people. When we returned to school the following Monday and discussed the causes of the weekend's tension and violence, we all seemed to agree on two main points. First, they believed as I did, that such violence and hate is contrary to the reaction of civilized men, that people today should be able to understand one another by means other than force. The second and perhaps the most important thing we all understood was that some day human beings will be able to live together and know one another as equals."

After other members of the class had spoken, I was introduced as the guest of the students: "Some people accept life in a fatalistic and a defeatist way. These people say, 'This is the way it was and this is the way it is and this is the way it will always be. Human nature cannot be changed. We have to be the way we are.' I shall never forget a girl in school who, when she did not do so well, said, 'Well, that's the kind of person I am. I can't do any better.' Well, I do not think you are going to be that kind of people. You are going to believe that the world can be different and that you can decide what to make of yourselves and how to affect the world you live in. This is humanism. Humanism is a faith in other persons as well as yourself.

"Our problem is to find out what it means to be a true human, an adequate member of the human species. A fox is true to his nature. A bear and an eagle act in accordance with their natures. So also a rabbit and a lamb. But what does it mean to be a man? Animals do not kill needlessly. They kill for food or in a fight for a mate. They do not torture. They are not needlessly cruel. They do not destroy in each other the will to live. But we humans are worse than the animals. And we have the intelligence and the ethical sensitivity to know better.

"Now when we are discouraged about people, when we begin to give up hope, we must remember that man is a complicated form of life. And man was a long time coming. It took millions of years for man to develop in the evolutionary process. And all that he had was two hands and feet and a brain. With these he walked this little planet in the midst of snakes and wolves and tigers. Without science or machines or guns man was able to stand against these wild animals and predatory beasts. He won out by his brain and his capacity to cooperate. He had no police or armies to protect him. Man learned to discriminate between food and poison, between animals that could be domesticated and those that must be hunted and kept at bay. And man created communities and institutions and government and culture.

"Humanism is a perspective on man's long history and his capacity for mastering the conditions of his existence. He can live with what he knows and what he does not know. He can learn. He can make choices of the kind of being he wants to be and the kind of world he wants to shape.

"One of man's problems has to do with identity. Many of us in the modern world have become confused about who we are and what we are. Each of us came from a particular ancestral background. One is Catholic, another Protestant, another Jewish or Hindu or Buddhist. Besides the religious ancestry, we have a nationality back of us—for even though we are Americans we can trace our past and our families back to Ireland, England, Russia, Germany, Africa, et cetera. It is important to know and be secure and proud of our past, but it is important to know something more: that you and I are not just creatures of our pasts. The important thing is not only where we came from but where we are going. What larger human reality are we part of? What do we mean by identification with the human community?

"We can identify with something much broader than nationality or race or class or a particular ancestry. We have ties which bind us—more than a particular group, more than black or white, rich or poor, male or female. We are Americans, including all cities and rural areas and sections of this great land. And more than that, we are members of the human species, the human family, the world community.

"Some people do not like what they are. They reject themselves and their backgrounds. 'Why do I have to be black?' asks the Negro child. 'Why do I have to be a Jew?' asks another child. There is fear and guilt among many whites. Many are troubled about their nationality and their ancestry in America and other countries.

"But our problem is to be what we are and to live where we live and to make our life something we can believe in and be proud of.

"I hope you will be glad to have been exposed to many religions and philosophies and faiths. I hope you will respect and understand that some of us are struggling to clarify and develop a humanist philosophy and an ethical judgment and a commitment to human potentialities as the heart of man's spiritual problem. I hope you will be able to say, 'When we were young there was great trouble in the world, but in all the confusion and violence we were exposed to many kinds of people and many approaches to life, in an educational process which made for fair play and decency and hope.'

"There is a story that long ago there were people who suffered slavery and exploitation and persecution. Nevertheless they believed that justice and decency and goodness must exist somewhere. When they could not find that in their lifetime anywhere in the world, they came to believe in a life after death. They made a commitment to each other: that when any individual died and came before the throne of the Most High, he would say to the judge, 'Please do not judge me alone, or at this time. Do not judge me by myself. Judge me and my life when all my people are here, and then let us all be judged together. I want to be judged as part of my community, my people, my generation.'

"In a way we are going to be judged whether we like it or not, by history; not individually, but as a people, as a people who had responsibility for human life. The important question is: will we live up to our own principles? Let us draw on the best in the human heritage of wisdom, in the democratic ideals of freedom and equality, in the great struggle for peace.

"It is the good fortune of the human race that great men appear out of the human community, men who embody whatever is good and true and beautiful. Sometimes such a man has to pay a price, even with his life, for what he stands for. But the hope is that we will learn from his sacrifice. We may be quickened by the death of such a man. His death may be the beginning of a new life for others in the generation to come. Martin Luther King touched many lives, more than most men. He touched them with the fire of a dream of a world without violence, a world of love, a world of equality."

What Is the Meaning of Ethics?

In the senior high-school class at Fieldston, the students challenged me. When we got all through talking about ethical issues, they asked, "Can you explain what you mean by ethics?" At a number of graduations I have used the basic approach I made that day.

How can we live together when we are so alike and at the same time so different? The differences arise not just from the fact that every one of our millions of cells is our own, and that in each of us all the chemicals and parts are combined in unique ways; they arise also because from the moment we are born each of us has his own experience. We see things differently. We develop our own attitudes and ways of thinking, feeling and acting.

In addition, every society is different, every community and every culture. The Navajo, Iroquois, and Sioux, the African cultures and Asian cultures, are all different. Their dances, their songs, their cultures and ways of life are different. The ethical question is, how shall people see one another, value one another, treat one another? We all recognize that there are different ways by which people relate to one another, different levels of human relationships.

Imagine that I show you five colors: yellow, orange, red, green, and blue. Your eyes see them, and the part of your brain that receives the message helps you to recognize and register the differences between the five colors.

Now I play five tones of music on some instrument. Your ear hears them, and the meaning and difference between the tones register in some part of your brain, and you know that they are full or half tones or even quarter tones, or maybe thirds and fifths apart. You may even have absolute pitch and be able to tell me exactly what the notes are. You have experienced color and tone through your eye and your ear and the part of your brain that enables you to recognize differences.

Can we in the same way recognize and identify five different levels, ways of people relating to one another?

The first: I don't like your face. I don't like the shape of your skull or your face or your nose; I don't like your hair. I don't like your religion, your color, your nationality or politics or anything about you, and I am going to kill you. We are not going to live in the same world if I have anything to say about it. We eliminate the people we don't like. The first level is: to kill; extermination.

Second level: I won't kill you. I'll let you live, but I'll use you. So long as you can be of use for my pleasure and profit and power, I will let you live. So thousands of years ago people, instead of killing their enemies, let them live; they made slaves of them. They used them as chattels, as their property. So the second level is: to use people; exploitation.

The third level: I won't kill or use you. I'll let you live, but don't come near me. I don't see any good in you. Stay out of my sight. I refuse to live with you, study or play or work with you. Stay on your side of the railroad track, your side of the wall, your side of the ocean. Some people might say this third way is pretty good; it's better than exterminating and exploiting people. It sounds good—"live and let live," at least we tolerate people and are tolerated. Yes, but it is a negative toleration, rejection, segregation, separateness. Suppose I said that I had the most wonderful marriage in the world: "My wife and I, we tolerate each other." Suppose I said, "This is a wonderful school, the teachers tolerate the children. The boys tolerate the girls. They don't kill or use them, but they don't see any good in them. They stay away from them." This is a negative kind of toleration, toleration with blindness.

The fourth level: Differences don't have to divide us. They can attract us, draw us together. Differences can be interesting, exciting, and provocative. I want to know you. I would like you to know me. If we try to know and understand each other, we might learn some things we don't know; we might grow. Each of us might become a bigger person. In a family every member is different. In a class every student is different. The same is true in a community. This fourth level is appreciation. It does not mean we have to be alike. You are different. You think differently. So do I. Appreciation is toleration with a positive note—not blindness, but a desire to see, to know, to understand, and to enjoy.

The fifth level: suppose we go beyond appreciation. What about us living, studying together, playing and working together? We might challenge each other. We might enlarge each other's lives and ways of looking at things. It wouldn't always be easy or comfortable or quiet. But it surely would be interesting, maybe exciting. We would stimulate each other, and each of us would grow. Imagine this between a husband and wife. Parents and children. Teachers and children going to the same school. People working together or facing common community challenges. This would be the creative level of relationship.

Now I ask you: do you grant that there are these different levels in the ways that people can relate to one another? Do you feel that these differences are real, or just imaginary? Can we agree that extermination, exploitation, toleration with blindness, appreciation, and the mutually creative relationship are on different levels?

I have not asked you to say which color is best, or to make a judgment on which tones are best. But now I am asking you to make your own judgment. What is a good life? What kind of relationships would you like to have in your life? What kind of relationships would you like to see in the community in which you live?

When you think about it, you know very well that there are not just five levels of relationships, any more than there are just five colors or five tones of music. There is a whole rainbow of colors, and a tremendous range of notes in music. Just so, there are thousands of ways of relating to people. On the negative and destructive side, you can kill with a weapon; you can also kill a person by starving him or overworking him. You can so discourage him that he has no will to live and kills himself. You can also rob and cheat a person, or lie and destroy his reputation and his good name. You can close a door in his face, or build a wall against him and say "Stay out! Stay out of my school, my community, my city, my nation." You can deny people jobs and housing. You can reject and humiliate them. You can say, "You're not as good as I am. You're not good. You're no good!" These are just a few of the negative levels. On the other hand, you can help a person to live and to want to live: care about him, heal him, teach him, encourage him, and get him a job. Open doors for him, expose him to all kinds of enjoyment and enrichment. You can appreciate him. You can stimulate and bring out the powers and talents in him. And you can love. There are thousands of ways of relating on the positive side, creatively, on the upper levels.

Every society, from the very beginning of human life, developed customs and a moral code of what was right and what was wrong, what was permitted and what was forbidden, what was expected of a person and what he could expect of others. It was necessary to have a moral code on many things. In almost every society at some time the moral code changed. Somebody said, "It isn't good enough; it's unfair; it's destructive; it's wrong." The practices of cannibalism, of slavery, of child labor, of inequality among races and nations and sexes, the exploitation of working people, the seizure of land from others, the killing of people in revenge and in war—these were accepted in many of the moral codes. But as time passed some people developed a conscience. They began to be troubled and to question and outgrow the moral codes of their childhood. They did not just accept and believe and conform, but they transcended the moral code. That is what we are living through now. Can we give support to the upper levels, the creative levels? Or must there be destruction? One way is the way of death—the death of the human. The other is a way of life—the birth and fulfillment of the human potentialities for greater health and creativeness, a more just and loving human world.

MARRIAGE

Introduction

It is hard to imagine human beings living in a society without families and homes. Revolutions in technology and in political and economic institutions may come and go; wars, civilizations, and religions may be born and die, but the human need for some form of family life continues.

Whatever the defects in family life, no form of human relationship or institution has done so much to safeguard and nourish the human element of the human being. And whatever forms marriage has taken in different cultures, it has helped to channel the powerful and life-giving sexual needs and drives. Marriage has proved to be the relationship in which love and trust can best grow between a man and a woman, and in which children can be brought into the world and cared for. Marriage provides the basis for making a home: a center for intimacy, privacy, and mutual aid, a place for sharing and love.

Making a marriage is one of the major decisions of our lives. We do not decide to be conceived and born. We do not choose our parents or our family. In the early years we have little to say about the influences that play upon us and shape our lives. Only with time do we become aware that we might select the influences and environment according to the way we want to live and the kind of person we want to be. In the matter of love and marriage it is crucial that we have some choice and control.

Throughout most of human history and in most cultures, the age of marriage, premarital conduct, choice of mate, and the nature and form of the ceremonies of marriage have been determined by tradition and custom. Today, and especially in the Western world, increasingly the young not only choose their mates but decide when and where and how they marry. In part, these ceremonies express a turning away from the authority of family and traditional religious institutions, a rejection of parental controls and a rejection of sectarian identities and the supernatural doctrines of traditional religion. Many couples wish to marry without theological or metaphysical beliefs and without mythologies and supernatural symbols. Many are without any religious affiliation or any clear affirmative philosophy and faith. For the most part they are agnostics and open-minded people who know more clearly what they do not believe than what they do believe about life, values, purpose, and meaning. They do not wish to submit to rituals which have no meaning for them. They reject the formality and the repetitious and impersonal character of traditional and conventional weddings.

The wedding is a public announcement of a marriage. The marriage is recognized and registered legally. The wedding marks a change in status for the man and the woman. Publicly, they are now the makers of a home and a family. But the act of joining their lives is their own. No state or church or other external authority can marry them. Nobody can marry them but themselves. It is what they feel in their hearts, and what is in the hearts of those whose lives are linked with theirs, that makes the true meaning of the wedding. In keeping with this spirit, I do not use such phrases as "By the authority vested in me . . ." or "I now pronounce you husband and wife." This spirit is best expressed in some of the selections from wedding ceremonies which are contained in the following pages.

Flowers and music, food and wine and dancing can help make a wedding a happy occasion. The place may be anywhere—a home or a hotel ballroom, a back-yard garden or a rooftop, backstage in an empty theater or in the warden's house at a prison. It may be in a garden or a field on a farm. If the place has simplicity and beauty and has positive associations, it can add to the mood and meaning of the experience. Privacy and quiet are important for the ceremony, for the concentration of feeling and the deep sense of communion. For many today, that meaning is no longer localized in a traditional prayer or creed and symbol. The words spoken can help direct emotion and clarify thought. But people, and especially the young, create the values and the meanings that sanctify their lives.

If a man and woman stand up together before their families and friends, join hands, and then walk out together in silence, this in itself may stir the deepest feelings. It will be a symbolic act of commitment to a life together. Those who love them will be sharing their moment of happiness and their hopes for the future. Some will be thinking of their own marriages, and others will be moved by thoughts of what the young couple will have to work out and live through. Some will be concerned about the hazards of the world that the couple will have to face in making a home and a family. Such feelings and thoughts can make the wedding an experience, beautiful and memorable.

When I have told couples that I believe no one can marry them but themselves, I have asked them if they would like to speak at their wedding, interpret what they mean by their marriage. Most of them have declined for various reasons: they have hesitated to express their most intimate feelings in the presence of their families and friends, or they have not trusted themselves to be able to do so at the time. They have felt they would have enough excitement and tension on their wedding day without adding to it or complicating the occasion. Some young couples have offered suggestions of favorite poems or passages from literature, or their own personal interpretations of marriage, with the hope that I would use them in the ceremony. Those who have taken responsibility for marrying themselves have for the most part spoken with sincerity, simplicity, and originality. The experience for those present has been one of memorable beauty. When couples have indicated to me that they want me to conduct the entire wedding, I have tried to make certain that each ceremony is personal and different.

The wedding ceremonies of Humanism are not uniform. They are all different, according to the personalities of the bride and groom, their background and education, whatever is unique about their shared and diverse interests, and the relationships with their families. The weddings are alike in that there is no reference to sectarian theology or religious beliefs or symbols. They are alike, too, in their emphasis on human values and the relationships which have to do with love, a home, family, and relationships to the larger human community.

A wedding doesn't make a marriage. Unless the relationship has the elements out of which a true marriage relationship can grow, the ceremony will have been a performance without meaning. After the last echoes of the music have faded away and the lights are extinguished and the guests have departed, what remains for the couple is the sense that "we are married." The aloneness with togetherness is real, as is the supportive and loving spirit of those who were present. One hopes the spirit of the ceremony will be with them all the years of their lives.

The marriage process actually begins when two people meet, become attracted to each other, and begin to explore who they are and where they came from and how they might live together. These considerations are part of the process of growing together. The wedding ceremony may set a seal on a marriage which has had its truest and deepest beginnings long before, and which will continue long after.

"Till Death Us Do Part"

They sat at opposite ends of the sofa. She was blond, Protestant; he was dark-haired, Jewish.

"We want you to marry us. We want to know what you are going to say at our wedding."

"Before we talk about that, I would like to know why you have come here. Why not a church or a temple?"

"We came because we aren't religious the old way," the young man said. "I can't go along with Christian beliefs. And my fiancee can't accept Jewish beliefs. We think that you 'can solve our problem."

"Why don't you go to a judge or a justice of the peace or the city clerk?"

"Look! We want *you* to marry us. Now, what will you say?"

"I can't tell you. We have no fixed ritual. Each ceremony is different and personal."

Now he was becoming impatient. He pressed me belligerently. "We want to know what you will say at our wedding!"

He was trying my patience. I said, "Why are you pressing me? Is something bothering you?" My voice rose. "You must have something in mind."

"Yes," he said. "I want to know if you say 'until death us do us part.

Now I was getting my tension up too. "I don't happen to use that phrase. But what's the matter with it?"

"I don't want to say it. It makes everything too final. How do I know I'll want to live with her six months from now?"

I said, "I'm not asking you to get married. You don't have to get married. But if you do get married, that's a serious matter, a life decision. You will be standing up before your families and friends and making a commitment to each other. And whether you use the phrase 'until death us do part' or not, you will be taking responsibility for your life together. Many marriages have trouble. Some fail. But whether it works out happily or not, it should be your intention to love each other and adjust to each other and try to make it work. The marriage is a legal contract as well as a personal decision, and it should be your purpose to live together as husband and wife all the years of your life."

The young man still seemed uneasy and disturbed. "Look," I said, "suppose I don't say anything at your wedding. Suppose you are the one to say what you mean. What would you say?"

After a few moments of silence, he said, "I love Mary. I can't live without her. I want her to be my wife."

"Fine! You have said three wonderful sentences. Will you say them at the wedding?" Now I was matching his impatient and belligerent voice.

"Yes, I'll say them!"

I turned to Mary. "What will you say, Mary?" She started to cry. I said, "You needn't say anything if you don't feel like it. I'll ask if you feel the same. How's that?" She nodded.

The date was set for the wedding—two weeks later on a Friday afternoon at five o'clock, in my office. In a more relaxed mood I asked, 'What is your work? What do you do for a living?"

He answered, "I'm a viola-player."

Somewhat imitating his pressure on me, I now pressed him. "Are you a good viola-player?"

"I'm the best viola-player in the world," he stated.

I said, "If you're the best viola-player, then I'm Jesus Christ!"

He laughed. "But I *am* the greatest."

After I had explained the procedure for obtaining a marriage license, the couple left. I must admit I wondered about the soundness of the marriage.

Two weeks later, at the appointed time, the couple arrived. They sat down on the sofa, just as they had at our first session. Three older couples arrived to participate as guests and witnesses. The three men were musicians—the leading cellist of the NBC orchestra and a cellist and violinist of the Philharmonic. The leading cellist was a very tall and heavy man with a deep, strong voice. His greeting to me and to the bride and groom filled the room.

"Are we all here?" I asked the groom. He nodded. I said, "I think we should begin. Will you stand up, please?"

The groom hesitated. "Couldn't we remain seated?"

The big cellist boomed, "Stand up!"

When we were standing together, I nodded to the groom. Very quietly he said, "I love Mary. I can't live without her. I want her to be my wife."

Turning to the bride, I said, "Mary, do you feel the same?"

Mary said, "Yes."

I said, "You are now husband and wife."

After the bride and groom exchanged rings, the big cellist asked in his booming voice, "Is that all?"

I said. "Thev want a sirnnle and short ceremony. They don't want me to make a speech and they don't need it."

"Make a speech!" boomed the cellist.

"I'll make a wish for them from all of us. It will be like a benediction from their families and all their friends." Then I said, "It is traditional to call down a blessing on you. But I say, bless you one another. It is your love that gives this marriage a promise of happiness and the power to work out a good life together. We wish that whatever difficulties you may ever have in your life, you will overcome them better because you share the burdens and care about your life together. And may all your joys be greater because you share them together. May you never rob each other of the taste for life but always, through the home and family you create, may you feel more zest for life. And above all, may you know peace and fulfillment through all the years."

No sooner was the ceremony over than the young husband motioned me over to the window in the corner of my office. He brought the big cellist with him. Waving his hand toward the cellist, he commanded, "Ask him! Ask him!"

For a moment I was puzzled. Then I recalled our initial conversation. Turning to the cellist, I asked, "Is he a good viola-player?"

The big cellist put his arm around the young man, and in his most resonant bass voice he said, "He's the best viola-player in the world!" That Sunday *The New York Times* carried the story and photograph of a famous string quartet playing a concert in the nation's capital on the hundredth anniversary of the birth of a world-renowned composer. The viola-player was our young friend.

Is It "For Real"?

One day a young man appeared and asked for information about the Ethical Culture Society and the Ethical Movement. "How did you happen to hear about us?" I asked. He answered, "I am a law student. In our study of marriage law, I came across the New York State Law of Domestic Relations. Apart from marriages performed by judges and justices of the peace, the law reads, in the section on religious marriage: 'Religious marriages may be performed by duly ordained clergymen and Leaders of the Ethical Culture Society.' It made me curious; that's why I'm here."

Wedding services conducted by Leaders of the Ethical Societies in New York State or by Leaders, even though from out-of-state, who are members of the Fraternity of Ethical Leaders of the American Ethical Union are recognized as legal by legislative enactment in New York. In some states the;; are so recognized by the liberal interpretation of the word "religious" or "ministry."

Years ago, at a very formal wedding, the father of the bride appeared in the full regalia of a high-ranking officer of the United States Navy. I believe he was a rear admiral. He bowed stiffly when we were introduced, and asked for my credentials, as if I were a naval officer reporting aboard his ship and expected to hold a certain rank and the right to perform certain functions and hold certain authorities. I laughed and almost saluted. "I carry no credentials with me, sir," I said, and we let it go at that.

I would like to add a word concerning the implications of the marriage license. It must be filled out and signed by two witnesses and the person conducting the wedding service. When it is sent in to the town or city clerk, or the marriage-license bureau, it becomes part of the official registry of marriages in the state. If there are never any questions concerning the marriage and the family, it may never be consulted. But the day may come when one or both parties may need proof that they were married and the details of when and where and by whom. This can involve people living abroad, problems of pass-ports, inheritance by children, and various types of benefits. I re-member when the widow of a war veteran appealed to me to help her prove to the Veterans' Administration that she really was the wife of her husband. The VA official in charge had never heard of the Ethical Culture Societies, and it took some doing to present him with evidence that he could accept.

Because the marriage license can be important, care must be taken to make sure all the details are handled correctly. This can sometimes confront those who have the responsibility of conducting marriage ceremonies with a dilemma. The following story is a good example of what can happen.

A beloved granddaughter was to be married at 6 p.m. Her grand-parents outdid themselves in preparation for the wedding—flowers, candles, a special dinner, and the best of the old family silver on a table covering of lace from the old country. Sixty members of the family and friends were present and on time for the ceremony and a reunion.

When the groom arrived with his best man and father, I took him aside and asked for the marriage license. His face fell. "I left it in my other suit," he said.

"Is your home far from here?" I asked. "Could you send someone for it? Without the license there can be no wedding. The marriage wouldn't be legal."

"I live too far from here," he said. "We couldn't have the license before late tonight. Can't you marry us anyway?"

At this point both fathers appealed to me. "All the preparations have been made! These wonderful people, many of them elderly, have come a long way. It would be very embarrassing not to have the wedding now. You simply must marry them!"

"What can I do?" I asked. "According to the law of the State of New York, they have to have a license. As a religious leader of the Society for Ethical Culture I have the authority to sign the license, but I am accountable."

"Isn't there some way to do it?" asked the groom.

"Yes, there is. If you promise to come to my office tomorrow at ten in the morning with two witnesses, your fathers or two other people, I will perform the ceremony now. That's the best I can do."

"It's impossible," groaned the groom. "We have reservations on a plane for Bermuda. It leaves at ten in the morning."

"I suggest you change the reservations to later in the day. It's your only possible way of having the wedding ceremony here and now. I wish I could do more, but I am not a free and independent individual in this matter."

After a consultation by the fathers and the groom and bride, the plane reservations were changed. We proceeded with the wedding, much to the delight of a warm and loving company of old and young.

The next morning the bride and groom appeared at the appointed time. "Do you take this woman to be your wife? . . . Do you take this man to be your husband?" After the proper affirmations and commitments, both fathers, acting as witnesses, signed the license. The couple departed on their wedding journey with gratitude and joy and affectionate good wishes.

Years later, a monsignor of the Catholic Church was a guest and witness at a wedding ceremony in my office. When the ceremony was over, we spoke together of matters of common interest. "By the way," I said, "have you ever had the experience of officiating at a wedding in which the groom came without his marriage license? And if so, how did you deal with the situation?"

The priest smiled. "It was very simple. I made it clear that I would perform the religious marriage on condition that the bride and groom would appear on the next day with the license for the legal ceremony."

I put out my hand. "Whatever our differences in theology, we seem to handle the practical the same way."

A Wedding That Flew Away

The girl was about eighteen, and four months pregnant. The boy was twenty-one. She was a Catholic, he a Lutheran. Both came from devout families.

"How did you happen to come to me?" I asked.

"In the place where I work, the woman in charge is a wonderful person," he said. "She saw that I was worried, so she asked to talk with me. I told her our story. I told her about the pregnancy. She said she listens to you on radio and she thought maybe you could help us."

"How do you know one another?" I asked.

"We live on the same block. We went to school together. We fell in love."

"Okay," I said, turning to the girl. "But you're pregnant. The first question I want to ask you is: would you want to marry if you were not pregnant?"

They looked at each other. She said, "That's not the reason at all. We would be married whether I was pregnant or not."

I said, "When you were together, didn't you have any idea that you could become pregnant? You look like bright people. Don't you know how babies are conceived and born? Did you just trust in the Lord?"

"Frankly," she said, "I didn't know much about it in the beginning. Then we thought we could get away with it."

"Didn't you know anything about birth control, about preventing a pregnancy?"

She said, "No, we didn't, and we still don't."

"Won't you agree that people should marry when they have the conditions and what it takes to help make a marriage work? And if you have a child, you should try to have it when you can really take care of it properly. You should want it and plan for it. It's too late for an abortion—even if you wanted it, you couldn't have it safely now. You could still have the baby and give it away for adoption. Because of the possibilities and because your decision about marrying now is so important for you and the child, you'd better talk to your priest and to the Lutheran minister. Try to get their advice before you decide anything."

The young man said, "Look, we want to get married. We want you to marry us. The priest wouldn't do it. My minister won't do it. She'd have to become a Lutheran. It's beginning to be evident that she's pregnant. Her mother's going to have a fit when she knows it. She's not a well woman."

Finally I said, "If, after you've had your talks, you still decide to marry and marry now, I'll conduct the ceremony."

For weeks I heard nothing. Then came an airmail letter from Florida. The young couple had decided to solve their problem by eloping. They flew away from both families. They felt more comfortable among strangers. A cousin who was friendly had responded on the phone to the effect that he would find them housing, a job, and someone to marry them. I still hear from them every year. They have a large family and are very, very happy.

When the Young Marry

When I ask, "Would you like to share in deciding the form and expressing the meaning of your marriage?" a few may say, as one couple did, "Here are the poems we love. We would be happiest to hear them at our marriage. They define so simply and so well the most undefinable idea in the world ... Of course, the decision of what to use, and where, and in what way, is ultimately yours."

They submitted the following selections.

> Bravest
> That has come my way:
> Loveliest
> That I have
> seen:
> Kindest, wisest, noblest—Be
> Noble, wise, and kind to me. . .
> .
>
> Do you love?
> Then, love are you
> —No other knowledge shall avail—
> To be, to know,
>
> And so to do,
> That is the truth, and all the tale:

So do, be so!
Immediately,
In each meridian and degree,
The Good, the Beautiful, the True
Is Love,
And Loving,
And is you.

. . . Give all thy love:
Love breeds its like always
—Spring-time,
And the moon,
And love—

Gentle,
Unasked
And truthful
—Such is love—
Compassionate
Is love,
And love
Is fruitful.

Making all song,
Making all creatures sing:
Surpassing all,

Staying
With everything:
Astonished all,
And all
Astonishing. . . .

More brave, more beautiful, and true
Than each one was
Is now this two. . .

Love!
It is to see,
And say:
You are best
Of all, I ween: . . .

—From James Stephens, "Theme and Variations"

An American Indian
Blessing

In one wedding in which the young people did not wish to speak,
they asked that I read a blessing from an unidentified American Indian

ceremony which meant a great deal to them. They had arranged that the wedding be held in a garden back of the bride's home in the suburbs. After my own statement on the meaning of love and marriage, I ended the wedding ceremony with the reading of their suggested blessing:

> Now you will feel *no* rain, for each of you will be shelter to the other.
>
> Now you will feel no cold, for each of you will be warmth to the other.
>
> Now there is no more loneliness.
>
> Now you are two persons, but there is only one life before you.
>
> Go now to your dwelling place, to enter into the days of your life together.
>
> And may your days be good, and long upon the earth.

The Young Speaking for Themselves

In the -presence of their parents and the two families and many young friends and fellow students, the hride, Elizabeth, and the groom, Peter, spoke informally. The wedding took place in the Ceremonial Hall of the New York Society for Ethical Culture. This was during the Vietnam war.

Peter: "Hello and welcome to our wedding.

"I would like to say a few words about what we think we are doing today.

"First of all, I want to say that when I first saw Elizabeth I said to myself, 'That's her.' I'd never seen anything like her. At first sight there she was, beautiful and sparkling, so alive and sensitive and exciting, I could hardly see anyone else. She was the only one present. It was a student party two years ago. Then it was the group that was taking over the student government at the college.

"Our revolution was not only successful politically, but this is at least the fourth marriage to grow out of it.

"In the year that I've been going out with Elizabeth and in the six months that I've been living with her, I've found that we have an uncanny ability to enjoy and be happy together. Our life has been a whirlwind of exciting experiences—hikes and ferry rides, the quiet enjoyment of the parks, doing really wonderful crazy things like going to a double feature, watching the life of the harbor, coming home in the wee hours or wandering down to Chinatown for a meal. It seems that no matter what situation we're in together, we're always enjoying it together and having the time of our lives. Then one day we found out that we had gotten into something really serious. We hadn't talked about it much. One of the first clues we had was when we saved money on a joint student membership at an art museum by joining as husband and wife. Elizabeth kept taking out her membership card, which said Mrs. Peter Swift. We really liked the sound of it.

"So here we are, announcing our commitment to each other and making official what is already a fantastic relationship. These are far from the best times in which to begin our Elizabeth-and-Peter joint enterprise. The first wedding present I received was a letter from my draft board ordering me to report for a physical. If the Army is so foolish as to decide that I am qualified to fight, Elizabeth and I will be starting our married life in another, less aggressive country. In any event, I am certain of one thing: that we are going to have a happy and exciting life together.

"I love Elizabeth very much and I've never been as sure of anything that I've done in my life as I am sure of what I am doing today."

Elizabeth: "I haven't much to add to what Peter has said. I felt the same about him. So the one thing I feel most in my heart right now is this. I want to thank my parents for what they've done for me through the years. I want to thank Peter's parents for what they've given me in their son. He's the man I have wanted. And I know we ' will have a good life together.

"Most of all, I want to say how happy I am that you are all here to share our happiness, you, our families, our friends and fellow-students, and our special neighbors. You all are our special community. To have you with us at this time makes our marriage even more wonderful. And we both appreciate it especially because we are of different backgrounds and our shared unity means that we can be enriched by each other. I hope our marriage will help dispel fear and ignorance and prejudice in ourselves and in others. We hope we can help to solve some of the serious human problems of our generation and contribute to a more just and peaceful world."

I then spoke. "After such an expression of love and commitment and faith, I have only a few words to add.

"May you always have more zest for life, more joy in life.

"May your faith in yourselves and in each other bring you the power to overcome difficulties.

"And may your love enhance all your joys because you share them together."

Our Marriage
—Barbara and Stephen

The following service was written by a social worker and a teacher.

We choose:

To build together a life of meaning and purpose based on mutual understanding, support, help, concern, compassion, and the highest form of human cooperation—love.

Our hope and promise is our commitment to search for knowledge—knowledge of each other's reality and needs which we will use to solve the mutual problems we face as loving friends, husband and wife, citizens, workers, mother and father, in our lives, and in the lives of our families, our friends, and our world. With the confidence we gain from this knowledge, we hope to dispel fear, ignorance, and prejudice in ourselves and others.

We have learned that our interests, and those of ail people, are mutual. We understand that the problems we solve and the solutions we find will be helpful not only to us, but to all of our friends, our families, and to everyone we will ever meet or know.

This love we share, which is a way of thinking, we will contribute to building a peaceful world.

That we can do this together is our hope. . .

That we will do this together is our joy. . . .

Without love, this world will be full of darkness and hate because love lighting up things. . . .

A new day is born. No more darkness. Light sings all over the world.

Love and Necklaces

This was a ceremony -planned and spoken informally by Jim and Betty. Both families were present in my office at the Ethical Culture Society.

Jim : "Last night I was sitting on my bed in the room I have lived in most of my life. I was thinking of things—what to say to Betty, to you people, and to myself. Images kept coming up, images of the past and the future, images of people. I think I saw and understood something of my life for the first time. Betty, I think I met you in my mind long ago, long before I actually met you. I thought of the place and the spot in time when I first met you. Now I actually know you after some years and we are getting married. And I know that above all else in our lives, what is here is a family.

"All through history, tribes and clans have formed their own communities. Now we are starting our own community.

"I place this necklace of amber around your neck, Betty, as a symbol of our love, my love for you, as you will place your necklace round my neck as your symbol of love for me. It is our love which will influence each of us and both of us for a long, long time."

Betty: "I was thinking, too. I saw all sorts of images. I thought of music, I thought of writing, literary images and musical images. I think of our life and I think of creativity.

"As I thought about marrying, I thought of my image in groups. I realized that I had always been afraid of groups and communities. I realized that I had been afraid of groups most of my life, when I was very young and again at college. I'd never been in a group. Like Jim, I wanted to be myself, an individual. I didn't want to have to conform, wear the same clothes, boots, make-up, and hairdo, or think and feel and act like others. With Jim I could be an individual, and he with me, because we were together. He helped me learn how to be an individual in a group. We are ready to be a community with others.

"We are not wearing wedding rings. I will wear Jim's necklace and place a necklace around his neck as a symbol of our bond and our love. If ever I am made uncomfortable or embarrassed because I am not wearing a ring, I may go out and buy one for myself. But I know that this necklace means marriage to Jim and me and those who know us. We are glad that you are here to share this day with us."

I concluded: "Jim and Betty, you have expressed deep feeling in simple words. You have shared your feeling of love with us, with those of us who love you and are a part of your life as you are part of ours. A wedding can be very elaborate and impressive, even extravagantly so. But your simple wedding is honest and beautiful. We who share it with you will always remember it. A wedding ring may be a traditional symbol and a mark of marriage; it may be made of gold that is pure and beautiful and never tarnishes or rusts. But the ring does not make a marriage. It is your identity with each other, your caring, your commitment to take care of each other, that will make the marriage. We hope you will stand by each other in health and sickness, in easy times and hard times, in peace and war. We have faith that you will live together as equals, and creative beings. We hope you will have a family and make a home.

"Now on behalf of the larger community of which we are all a part we recognize your right to use two names which are old and dear, to you the newest and dearest of names, husband and wife."

The Strength of Our Love

On a sunny afternoon in early June, in the shade of a young maple beside a clear, flowing millstream in Woodstock, two families and forty friends stood for the wedding ceremony. There were many children of friends and relatives, ranging in age from five months to five years, and there was the sprightly grandmother of the bride, aged ninety-four. Of all the varieties of costumes, the outstanding one was the bride's dress. It had been worn by the bride's grandmother, who had been born in frontier days on the plains of

Nebraska. The long, graceful gown was cream-colored, with a wide lace yoke, a touch of lace at the wrists, and a delicate gathering at the waist. The gown had served family weddings without requiring a stitch of alteration. The bride wore no jewelry. Her only ornament was a white flower at the back of her hair.

The bride and groom stood facing each other. The only person seated, and she sat right near them, was the grandmother, who listened intently to every word. The following words were written by the bride and groom, Susan and Art. At Sue's request, Art read them. When Art paused at one point in the reading and asked if Sue would read, she said, "No," and then kissed him.

"Sue and I and our families thank you for coming today. We wanted you to share with us this important day in our lives. For about one year now we have been seriously considering a marriage commitment to each other. We have lived together for two years, working at building a solid and loving relationship. There have been times when each of us has been discouraged, felt stymied or frustrated in our attempts to grow stronger individually and as a couple— but during these two years we have learned to cherish, support, and rely on one another.

"We have found that in many ways we are very different types of people. Sue is serious; I am often playful. Sue has long-range goals and enjoys planning for the future. My goals are short-range and I like to organize the present. Feelings of comradeship among friends are very important to me in determining my life style, while Sue is „ more needful of privacy. We appreciate these opposite qualities in one another for the balance that they give us. At the same time, we try to reach a common ground, and as a result we are teaching each other many important things. For example, Sue is teaching me to relax alone, and I am helping Sue to relax with others.

"In other ways we aren't so different. Our basic goals for our relationship are the same. We have certain qualities in common that we are proud of and both cultivate. We work to be considerate, supportive, and flexible, and try to be as honest about our feelings as we can without thoughtlessly hurting.

"The decision to get married was not an easy one for us to make. We felt none of the external pressures that often push other couples toward marriage, and both of us were frightened by marriage. Marriage involves for us a commitment to do our best to satisfy fully our needs for each other, and to achieve greater intimacy. This is a difficult responsibility, but it is probably the most important reason that we are getting married. We have enjoyed two years of personal growth and growth together, and feel that marriage will further this growth, both as individuals and as a couple.

"Since the time that we started writing this ceremony back in December, the process of working out specific plans and all the things that led up to this wedding have intensified the feelings we have talked about here. In reading the ceremony earlier this week, we realized that we have lost most of our fears and gained even greater confidence in the strength of our love. We look forward with joy to our years together and see this wedding as a symbol of our promise to continue building a life together. We believe that we can do this well and bring joy to ourselves and those we love."

When Arthur finished his reading, I spoke of the importance of a home in meeting the deepest needs of the human being. I spoke of the families and friends who were sharing the wedding and whose love and wishes would follow the life of Art and Sue wherever their lives took them. Then Art and Sue repeated after me the words, "With this ring I thee wed, in love and truth, in joy and sorrow, through life." Both had trouble getting the rings on past the second joint of the third finger of the left hand. I commented that it was a sign that each of them would have to work at making the marriage.

The Wedding Bing

Some conventions remain, survivals from long, long ago. What are their origins? Some we know. Some are lost in the mists and mysteries of primitive experience and ways of seeing and interpreting nature.

Originally in some cultures the golden ring may have been an amulet to keep evil spirits and ghosts away from the loved one. In still other cultures it was protection against witchcraft or the evil magic of hostile people.

Did it come from the ancient practice of bride purchase? Was it the remains of a chain, a binding link? Is it a mark of possession dating from the days when women had subordinate status and even were considered possessions? Is it a notice to all men that this is somebody's wife or woman, a mark of taboo—this one is not to be touched by others?

Or is it the symbol of sealing a contract? A part of an exchange of gifts between the groom and the bride? In some cultures the ring was large and heavily carved and was used to stamp the contract in wax with the arms of a family, or it was a ring with a family history.

Shall we say today, whether there is one ring or two, that the husband and the wife are touched by the blessed power of the sun? The symbol of the sun with its light and warmth and life-giving power—the center of our solar system, the great orbit of the life of our planet earth.

Obviously, a man and a woman can be married without a ring. The ring does not make a wedding. Nor does the price and cost of the ring make a marriage. But the ring may be a symbol of love, of caring, of responsibility, and the uniting and binding of two lives.

The ring is a token of love, more than the gifts of preliminary courting and "engagement," a love commitment. Its circle unites, a more sophisticated interpretation—the circle without end, a relationship without end. The words said and the placing of the ring on the bride's and groom's fingers constitute a symbolic act which makes the bride a wife and the groom a husband.

"With this ring I thee wed, in love and truth, in joy and sorrow, through life. . . ."

How many times have I had to warn the groom: Don't try to force the ring onto your bride's finger! The ring, whether of silver or gold or other metals, whether ornate or simple, may fit perfectly in the jewelry store. It may fit perfectly five minutes before and five minutes after the wedding ceremony. But nine out of ten times, at the crucial moment in the wedding, it will not move beyond the second joint of the third finger of the left hand. Why that finger? Tradition holds that there is a special little artery that runs from the heart to the fourth finger.

Picture a formal wedding in a first-class hotel. Two hundred guests dressed in top style. The procession has brought the maid of honor, the best man, the bridesmaids and ushers into a proper and beautiful human constellation for the bride and groom. A solemn and affectionate and joyous interpretation of the meaning of the wedding is now to culminate as the groom places the ring on the bride's finger.

But the ring doesn't move past the second joint. The groom does not relax. He is determined. It seems more important to him to get that ring on all the way than it is to give attention to what he is saying: "With this ring, I thee wed. . . ." He forces the ring farther. He pushes and twists as if his life depended on it. The bride's face is strained, pained, then extremely agonized, and finally angry. She kicks the groom in his shin right in the middle of the wedding. Yes, it actually happened. The place was the Hotel Pierre in New York.

On a few occasions the groom has forgotten the ring. On a few occasions the best man has been late. In some cases the groom has lacked the money to buy a ring. Almost everyone who is called on to officiate at weddings has kept an extra wedding ring in his desk for emergencies.

Notes for a Wedding—I

Although each wedding has been personal and unique, according to the place and number of guests and the situation in which the bride and groom have found themselves, 1 have tended to gravitate toward the main ideas embodied here. I have often used variations of these passages and ideas where they seemed appropriate.

In the life of each of us there are a few days which are very special days. One of them is our wedding day. We call it a Golden Day. It is as if all our yesterdays were a preparation for this day, and as if all the tomorrows will be different and more meaningful and fulfilling. It is a day when for us the earth stands still, a day when the light of our happiness shines forth as we look at each other and commit ourselves to each other.

Those of us who know you and love you are glad that you found one another, that you love one another, and that you have decided to relate your loving to living in this marriage.

Marriage is a dedication. You give yourself, your life and love into the hands of the one you love. You do so trustingly and generously. By the same token, each of you receives a gift—the life and love of the other. You receive this gift not only from the one you love, but from the parents who brought you into the world and reared you, who dreamed of this day, and who are in a sense fulfilled in your marriage. And you receive this gift from the personal world of friends who are joined in friendship and faith in your marriage.

Marriage is a responsibility. It is a commitment to care for each other with all the tenderness and consideration of which you are capable, to stand by each other no matter what the days ahead may bring, of sickness and health, of the difficult as well as the easy, happy times.

To take on such responsibility for another life, to bind yourself, to carry such burdens might seem limiting and overwhelming, were it not for love. "Love" is a word often used with vagueness and sentimentality. We mean something very real. When we bind ourselves in love, it can mean sweet freedom and fulfillment. It can lighten burdens, making it a joy to serve each other.

When we love, we see things other people do not see. We see beneath the surface to the nature and gifts and temperament, the qualities which make this one different and dearer than all others. To see with a loving eye is to know the inner beauty. And to be loved is to be seen and known as we are known to no other.

Such love means security. Each of us would like to have an absolute security. This we cannot have. But we come close to it when we are loved, when another human being wants us, wants to share life with us, accepts us without qualification or reservation, not as perfect—but as human, with our strengths and weaknesses. To love is to give another human being a deep feeling of security and support.

The love of which we speak is not static. It is a growing and dynamic relationship. Each of us has a dream of himself as a better person. We think that tomorrow and tomorrow we will grow and fulfill our possibilities. It is a great blessing when someone believes in our dream of ourselves and wants to live with us and help make the dream come true.

One test of your marriage will be the way you affect each other, how you help each other grow, so that each is more fulfilled, each more of a person. Thus through your love you will stimulate and challenge each other and enlarge each other's world. You will never be smug or settle for too little. You will look forward to every day as a new day to be filled with living, and you will have zest for life. Life will never be dull or boring if, through your love, you live creatively with each other through all your years to the last breath.

Beyond all religious traditions, beyond all philosophies and cultures, love between man and woman is a profound spiritual experience. When you love you identify with one another, you sense each other's needs and moods without words. If the other suffers physical pain or some other kind of hurt, you suffer. If the one you love is happy, that is your happiness.

You will know this best when you have a child. If the child is sick or hurt, you suffer more than the child does. You would gladly take the pain upon yourself. So it is in love between man and woman. You live and die in one another. Such is a love of life-in-life.

Marriage means a home. Not something bought with money or made out of brick and stone, but a home which is a center for a quality of life, a way of life created out of your very selves. We hope that you will make a true home, a center and a base for both of you, for your sharing of life. And we hope that it will embody what you evoke as you share life together, your strength and your vitality, your intelligence and your love of books and music, your love of children and your love of people, your sense of humanity and your love of life.

It is our hope that your home will honor the best in the human heritage, that it will be a source of human understanding, for justice and peace in the larger community. May you always find rest there when you are tired, new strength when you are discouraged.

Because marriage is so intimate and permanent, you are more exposed and vulnerable than in most relationships in life. You can be ecstatically happy or utterly miserable. May your differences never divide you or blind you to the good in each other. May they be as nothing because of the love you bear each other. May you find patience and understanding and forgiveness in each other. Through our differences and the way we resolve and solve our problems, our love becomes deeper, our faith stronger.

May you never rob one another of the taste for life or the will to live. But always through your life together may you have more zest for life, more will to live, and more faith in yourselves and one another.

It is a tradition to call down a blessing, but it is your love and faith which consecrate this marriage.

Notes for a Wedding—II

I love you for what you are. I love you for what I am when I am with you.

With you I am alive. You have opened my eyes and unstopped my ears.

You have hung the stars in the sky and made the roses and irises to color the earth. You have filled my emptiness, my darkness, with light, radiant and golden.

Love takes time and grows deep.

Love goes through stages from innocence to awareness and maturity.

Love may begin physically and end intellectually and aesthetically and spiritually. It may begin spiritually, intellectually, or aesthetically

and end in full physical expression and fulfillment. But whatever way it begins and ends, it must be produced from the inner life and involve the heart as it moves toward another person. It is human beings sharing. It is someone moving toward someone. It is each as object and each as subject—both sharing together a movement toward light.

Dante said that love is the power that moves the earth and the planets and the sun itself.

Wedding on a Farm

Imagine a small farmhouse. In one of the meadows a
Siberian elm reached high above the -pines and spruces
that lined the old stone wall. The groom and the best
man stood with me at the base of the tree. Families
and guests were standing together with an aisle between
them for the bride. Under one of the maples the young
brother of the bride played a plaintive motif on his
flute while her father led her out of the old farmhouse
into the meadow to the side of the groom. Her father
kissed her and went to stand beside his wife.

The bride and groom were social workers, two young
black people who were devoting their talents and
professional competence to foster a better life for
children and youth in a community center in Boston.
Their influence had permeated the neighborhood with
hope and faith. And now their parents, aunts and
uncles, cousins, friends, and fellow staff members were
gathered to share their joy on the occasion of their
wedding. The gathering of black and white in the
meadow was as natural and warm as the good earth,
and as loving.

The young wife wrote to me some weeks after the
wedding.

"Dear Dr. Black:

"No doubt you have wondered why you have not heard from us as yet, not even a thank-you note.

"When Bob and I pulled away from the farm after we had become man and wife, I tried to reflect on the few hours before. ... I thought back on the ceremony: the flute music, the slope of the hill we walked down from the house, the rows of people standing and waiting before me, the serenity of the hills, the sunshine of the day. I tried to recall some of the words that you had spoken in the ceremony. I found, however, that I could not. Either they were too closely behind, or they had already become a part of me and were not yet settled inside. A phrase kept running through my head: 'and may your home become a center for a certain quality.'

"As I rode further in the car I began to realize that I was not yet ready to think about our wedding because it went so deep and so strong.

"A few days later we were on our honeymoon in New Hampshire. We were staying in a log cabin without water, electricity, or any of the usual conveniences of a house. It was chilly and we had to keep a wood fire burning all the time. We chopped wood, fetched water in buckets, read at night by candle and flashlight, and slept on the wooden floor before the fireplace in sleeping bags. The day, what we did, when we ate, when we slept, was all according to our whim and desire of the moment. No telephone, no doorbell, no one else. Here again I tried to think about our wedding. Again I could not.

. . . Why was it that I could not sit down with myself or with Bob

and talk about, even think about, that most important and meaningful and very beautiful day? Again I felt that the very fact that I
couldn't must have meant something and so I did not push it or force
it.

"Indeed it was not until tonight that something began to happen
inside me. Bob was at a meeting downstairs with some college
students and I was entertaining a young Puerto Rican housewife
from New York who had come with a friend to pick up some books.
She began to tell me why she sometimes denied the fact that she was
Puerto Rican because she did not always want to be so identified.
The phone rang occasionally. Bob came upstairs from the meeting to
get coffee for everyone, and the TV was on. A couple of times I got
up to check something that was cooking on the stove. Then another
person came upstairs to wait for Bob. The young housewife left with
her friend for New York. . . . The man waiting for Bob . . . We
talked about many things. . . . The phone rang again about a
meeting. ...

"Suddenly as we sat there something came alive inside me and I.
knew what you had meant: 'and may your home become a center for
a certain quality.' I felt that it was just that. That here in our
tenement apartment on Elbert Street in Roxbury, where outside the
window abandoned cars crowded the street, and broken glass littered
the sidewalk, and tiny tots roamed at night, here was where we
belonged. I knew all that in a moment, all in that moment. I knew
that I was not very happy about having to have our son live forever
on these streets. . . . But what I meant was that here in our home,

this small four-room apartment which was crowded and filled with books and magazines, paintings and records, African Freedom bells on the walls, piles of newspapers to be clipped, coffee jar on the table, and sketches and quotes on the walls, this was who we were and what we were. For each other a haven among it all. For others a door which would always be open for dialogue and laughter. Here was where ideas, feelings, pain, and joy would be shared. Here was where the revolution of our times would be planned as well as the revolution of our family, which itself was a great challenge in a sense anyway: to live as people and with truth and with love in spite of, and in concert with all else.

"And so you see, Dr. Black, here, at our home, was where the revelation and the image and the importance of our wedding ceremony came to me. Now the simplicity, the honor, the depth, and the beauty of it all I can see and feel and grasp. Our friends were there because they were people we wanted to be there, each with a special significance. Hank playing his flute because he wanted to give us that. Little Bob in the ceremony because he wanted to be. You performing and giving the ceremony because both you and we wanted you to.

"This is very meaningful for me to realize these things now, and I am glad that I could tell you.

"Thank you, Dr. Black, thank you."

Wedding in a Bistro

The locale was M.I.T. The catalyst was math. If it had not been for a common passion for numbers, addition and multiplication tables and equations, who knows whether they ever would have fallen in love?

They could have been married in the family's church or the bride's home. Instead, they chose a bistro. They wanted a serious Humanist wedding to be followed by a party for their families and their many friends, a party to end all parties. Where else but Basin Street East?

Tables were removed so that lots of people could see and hear the ceremony. The bandstand became an altar. The carpet which usually covered the area for those who hung around the bar was laid for the wedding procession. The red velvet rope which usually served to keep people in line marked off the bridal aisle. The couple wanted the ceremony to be dignified and solemn, as well as joyous and beautiful. No drinking or smoking beforehand. The bride wore a taffeta gown with imported lace, the groom a black business suit.

After I had spoken and the couple had exchanged rings, everybody kissed and embraced everybody else, including the bride and groom. Champagne flowed. Hot and cold canapes were available in ample quantities. No one received more tributes and toasts than the Basin Street Chinese chef, who outdid himself providing knishes and assorted delicacies. The jazz trio made loud and rhythmic music for dancing. Joining in the festivities was the bride, playing on her bass fiddle.

After about five hours of one of the liveliest and the gayest free-swinging parties ever seen in this bistro, the bride changed into dungarees and sweatshirt. The groom put on his jeans and heavy shoes. And the married pair headed for a honeymoon in West Virginia, for some mountain-climbing and cave-exploring. They carried mountain gear in their tiny Austin. A number of guests accompanied them, but only because this was their regular season for cave-exploring. The cost of the honeymoon was estimated at a total of $100 for two weeks. The bride's father smiled happily as he paid the very substantial bill for the party.

The Tree Full of Children

They were young city people, but they wanted their wedding in the country under a tree. What kind of tree? They didn't know. An impressive tree. So they prevailed on friends to let them have their fall wedding on the friends' property in New York State near Irvington-on-Hudson. It was held in an open field bordered by maples and evergreens. And although they were from the city, the young couple chose their tree almost instinctively. It was a white oak, the king of trees, that stood out above all the others in height and color, its green foliage tinged with red. It was an oak with an impressive and noble crown, with an almost mystic power, as if it were the embodiment of the essence of all that "treeness" can mean.

As I walked with the groom and best man toward the assembled guests at the edge of the wood, I was thinking of how best to express the spirit and meaning of the wedding in this setting. I was not prepared for what I saw as we approached the tree. Perched up in the branches were neighbors' children who had been drawn by the news of the wedding. For them it was something special, something of dramatic importance, a "happening." They were sitting, standing, and kneeling, high above us on the tree's branches.

As the bride and her bridesmaid joined us, the children kept a perfect silence. I do not recall the exact words I spoke in the wedding ceremony. Words were a small part of the total experience. I do remember, however, that I was moved to say that sometimes the natural beauty of the earth and the love of people for each other make us very glad to be alive. We are filled with reverence for life. In such moments we are able to love and be loved. And with such love we can share life and make a marriage and a- home and a family.

It was as if the ancient worship of the tree of life were part of this "rite of passage," for the bride and groom a communion of nature and human beings. Against the blue sky and the sunshine, the tree full of children was alive with color and light, and more beautiful than any stained-glass window in a cathedral.

Backstage in a Theater

I remember a wedding in a theater between a singer and a dancer in the musical *Pal Joey*. The ceremony was held on a Saturday afternoon between the matinee and evening performances. Two families gathered backstage as soon as the matinee audience cleared out. The cast, many with their make-up still on, and some in costumes which they thought might not be out of place, joined with musicians and stage manager and staff and stagehands.

The theater had been central to the careers of the young couple. They had met in the theater, and there they had fallen in love. A theater without audience and a stage without scenery can be cold and empty. But on that late afternoon between performances, something made the light and warmth unusual: unusual because the bride and groom were so handsome, talented, and happy; unusual because of the elements which are part of the life of those in show business; the precarious existence of theater people as plays come and go, the dependence on one another for timing and close teamwork in every performance, the competitiveness and the respect for talent and achievement—all these made for deep sentiment and identification to the point of sentimentality. I learned that even without words, music, and movement, a wedding in a theater can be a peak experience. And it is an "acting-out" that works better without an audience.

An Intermarriage in the Country

I remember another rural wedding. The groom was the son of an Italian Catholic family. The bride was Jewish, but Jewish by ancestry and identification only. Whatever the strength and weakness of the religious convictions of each of the two families, both of the young people were Humanists, agnostics, and intelligent, sensitive, and socially concerned young people.

When we met in my office to plan the wedding, our discussion ranged over a great many topics: their backgrounds, education, career interests, and the attitudes of the families. I gathered that both families were enthusiastic about the marriage, the Italians for their new daughter-in-law-to-be, and the Jewish family for their new son. Here was something to look forward to. The young man said, "We want the wedding to be out of doors, in the country. My family has an old-fashioned Italian restaurant and some farmland about 130 miles north of the city near the New York and Connecticut border." We set the ceremony for a Sunday afternoon in June.

On the appointed day, I arrived at the restaurant and then took the road that led into the gardens and open fields adjacent to the main house. On the way I passed gardens filled with flowers and vegetables: lettuce, tomatoes, zucchini, finocchio, celery, and radishes. Near the farmhouse, on the lawn, were set out sixty chairs with a central aisle ending at a small table with a linen runner and large vase of flowers. At the other end of the lawn, at the edge of the meadow, were tables stacked with food, Italian cuisine on one side,

Jewish on the other: salami, varieties of antipasto, cheeses, anchovies, breads, and wines; also cakes, fruits, and coffee brewing Italian style. On an equal number of tables were knishes, rice, sour cream, herring, cucumbers, onions, sliced cold salmon and bagels, and kosher wine.

In the main house, the groom greeted me and introduced me to the two fathers. We sat down then and there and signed the license so that we would not have to think about it in the excitement of the wedding party after the ceremony.

The families had met one another previously. Now, when guests began to arrive, there were no cool, formal handshakes; there were embraces and warm smiles. In the background one could hear Neapolitan songs played by an accordionist. When all had arrived, it was not easy to break up the socializing, but the sixty guests took their seats, the music ceased, and down the aisle walked the two young people, holding hands, she dressed in a white bridal gown and he in a dark suit. In the silence it was just a walk in the sun. The two families followed them with their eyes, as if they were both the children of a single family.

In my ceremony I stressed the theme that the more we love, the more we can enjoy nature's gifts, and the more we love, the more we can be enriched by what human beings have brought forth through human talent and creativeness. When we overcome the barriers of religious and national prejudice, we can be enriched by the great variety of the traditions and cultures of the world, the achievements of the past and those that are still to be.

The spirit in the people present was infectious. It was as if they were part of the warm sun and the blue sky, the flowers and the rich foods, and the green grass underneath. It was as if all of them were being married. They were dancing inside even before the dancing began. When the ceremony was over, they came forward to embrace the couple. Then the drinking began, with many toasts between the families and then a line-up at the food tables so that they could serve themselves and then sit down at the tables that had been prepared for them. Italian music and dances, Jewish music and Jewish dances, the feasting and the toasting, went on and on as the sun sank. The guests lit the little lamps on their tables. I made the rounds and offered my good wishes and made my farewell. As I drove away, the lights on the tables and the music were a happy scene to remember. I remembered Dr. Elliott's words: "At a wedding a beautiful thing can happen."

The Zulu and the Greek

How should a bride and groom dress for a wedding? How should they dress if they are to be married in a garden? And what if it is a garden high up, overlooking the Hudson River, on a Saturday afternoon bright with the golden sun of mid-September?

When they came to see me for the discussion of their marriage and the wedding, both were dressed conventionally: he wearing a business suit, she a dress. The man, a member of the Zulu tribe in South Africa, was studying business administration. The woman, of Greek Orthodox upbringing and brought up in Turkey, was studying for her doctorate in education. Since neither was traditionally religious, it was easy to agree on a simple ceremony which would emphasize the common ground of faith in human values and human potentialities.

On the afternoon of the wedding, approximately a hundred people, members of families, fellow students, and friends drawn from various national and cultural backgrounds, gathered in the garden. The variety of costumes and the friendliness of the people evidenced a spirit and created an atmosphere that made one think of the United Nations.

When the wedding was about to begin, the ushers brought out two white ribbons and held them so that the wedding procession might have a lane through the guests gathered in the garden. I led the way through the lane with a small dark-haired Greek child, a nephew of the bride, gripping my hand tightly while in his free hand he held the two precious gold wedding rings. Behind us came the groom. He walked proudly, naked except for a loincloth made of zebra hide. His handsome body shone golden bronze in the afternoon sun. His head was topped by a turban of zebra hide, and on his left arm was a shield of the same zebra design. In his right hand he held a spear.

Behind the groom came the bride. She wore a long plum-colored gown reaching to the ground. Her lovely face was framed by long brown tresses and around her throat hung a brilliant blue turquoise necklace sent especially by the Zulu people in honor of the occasion. Behind her walked two little nieces dressed in green velvet dresses and scattering rose petals over her. When the wedding procession arrived at the end of the garden, the ushers removed the two white ribbons. The guests gathered round the bride and groom.

In such a gathering of friends from many parts of the world, it was easy to experience a hope and faith in the human community. There was a respect and joy in the joining of two lives beyond the differences of religion, nationality, and culture. AH shared in a sense of the binding and liberating force of love. Each in turn repeated after me, he in Zulu and she in Greek, the following:

"Because I know the good in you, the one I love, I know there is good in life. You give me faith in life.

"Because you have chosen me, to love me and live with me in this marriage, I know there is good in me. You give me faith in myself." When they had made their commitment to each other and each had placed the ring on the finger of the other, they kissed. I quoted from Euripides' *Medea:* "Surely this doth bind through all ill days, the hurts of humankind when man and woman in one music move." Then Zulu drums and Zulu songs filled the air. In the midst of the toasts and the mixing of guests of many nations, one man said, "I've seen many brides that were underdreissed, but I've never seen such a naked groom."

Yes. But because the newlyweds held to their traditions, the many costumes and customs added beauty and taste. They shared a profound spiritual experience of commitment to each other and their respective families and ethnic backgrounds and cultural values. They were part of a world which is coming into being, a world of pluralism and of human understanding and cultural enrichment.

A Wedding in Two Languages

At the wedding of a young Mexican artist and an American girl, the two families were present, hut the Spanish-speaking Mexican family spoke no English. To conduct the entire marriage service in English would be, it seemed to me, meaningless for them and an affront. Accordingly, I asked the groom to make his

commitment in Spanish, and the bride, in English.

When this had been made clear, the Mexican family, which had been formal and distant, smiled and evidently felt they had become an integral part of the wedding party.

Since then, on a number of occasions when the bride and groom have been of different national and cultural backgrounds, I have suggested the use of two languages in the ceremony. The languages, a combination of English with Italian, Hebrew, French, and Russian, and of Zulu with Greek, have added beauty

and color and a dramatic quality, and have heightened
the awareness that this new family and this home
will reap the benefit of two traditions and identities.
The languages have expressed a respect and have
drawn families and friends together in a spiritual
bond of solidarity and communion.

The following service, in English and in Spanish,
conveys the flavor of the ceremony.

May you always be able to say, "Because I know the good in you, the one I love, I know there is good in life. Because you have faith in me and join your life with mine, I know there is good in me."

May you never rob one another of the faith in self and in the other. May you so live together that you always enhance each other's taste of life, will to live, and faith in life.

It is traditional to call down a blessing upon you. But it is your faith and love which make this marriage sacred. In this spirit, and with a deep sense of commitment:

Do you take this woman to be your wedded wife?

Do you take this man to be your wedded husband?

Now, repeat after me: "With this ring I thee wed."

Now then, in the presence of your families and friends, and in the sight of the community of mankind of which we are all a part, you have the right to use two names which are old and dear and sacred in the life of the race—to you, the newest and dearest of names—"husband" and "wife."

Podrdn Ustedes siempre decir, "Porque conozco la bondad en ti, la persona que amo, yo se que bay bondad en la vida. Porque tienes fe en mi, y unes tu vida a la mia, yo se que hay bondad en mi."

Que nunca robe uno al otro la fe uno misma o en el otro. Que vivan juntos de una manera que aumenten en cada uno el -placer de vivir, el deseo de vivir, y la fe en la vida.

Es tradicional bendecirlos. Pero en verdad, es su fe y su amor los que hacen sagrado este matrimonio. En este sentido y con una 'profunda dedicacion:

Acepta Usted tomar a esta mujer per esposa?

^Acepta Usted tomar a este hombre por esposo?

Ahora—repita despues de mi: "Con este anillo te caso."

Ahora en la presencia de su familia y sus amigos, y tambien en la presencia del genero humano de que somos todos parte, Ustedes tienen el derecho a usar dos nombres que son muy antiguos y sagrados en la vida de la raza—pero ahora a Ustedes los nombres mas nuevos y mas queridos—los nombres—"esposo" y "esposa."

A Few Dilemmas

The performance of a professional service often presents ethical problems. As this is true for the physician, lawyer, teacher, and engineer, so it is true for the priest, rabbi, and minister, and no less so for those who function as Leaders of the Ethical and Humanist Movements. For those who officiate at marriages, there are sometimes particular dilemmas. It is difficult to refuse to officiate, even when one has strong doubts concerning the marriage of a couple. If we believe that love between people is the most important thing in life and if we wish to encourage and support those who wish to take responsibility for their love and join their lives in marriage, how can we refuse to serve them? Sometimes our uneasiness has to do with our sense that we may be party to a marriage which is bound to run into serious trouble and will probably fail, with the failure causing suffering and tragedy for those concerned. The judgment is not made easily. But many will say that this is not the responsibility of the judge or justice of the peace or the priest, rabbi, or minister. People have to be free to make their own life decisions. This means that they have the right to make their own mistakes. It sounds true and good, but what is the responsibility?

Responsibility to the couple who ask to be married? Responsibility to oneself and to the agency or institution or the movement to carry on certain professional services?

Example: a professional worker in the medical field brings a young girl to my office. Will I marry them right now? He is thirty-five and of Jewish ancestry, she of Spanish Catholic background. He says that she is eighteen years old. It is possible that she is eighteen. I find it hard to believe. I have to admit my skepticism may come from the fact that her English is not very good; she is quite inarticulate. But they have a marriage license. That means that the city clerk's office must have accepted evidence of her birth date. If she were under eighteen she would require parental consent. Is this the problem? Why do I hesitate to marry them? Is it because the man is twice her age, far more educated than she is, and they are of such different backgrounds, religions, family income, and cultural levels?

In our discussion of the reasons why they should and should not marry and why I hesitate to perform the ceremony and sign my name to the license, I am unable to elicit any satisfactory reason why her family is not present. If the parents exist, why haven't they come to their daughter's wedding? If they are working people, why can't they have the wedding in the evening? Why the rush to have it now? He says it is because he can take a short vacation now, his only chance. It becomes evident that they have been "living together." I ask if the girl is pregnant. The answer is no. He insists that he loves her. "It's a chance for a better life for her."

What is my responsibility—and to whom? To the girl? I have a private session with her, but she sticks to one statement: she loves him and wants to marry him.

Under pressure, I insist on time to think it over. Besides, I have a dozen matters I have to tend to. Our discussions have already taken precious hours of a workday. After a recess of about an hour, the man informs me that an older couple who are friends of both will be present to confirm all his answers to my questions and to try to allay whatever qualms I have expressed about the wisdom ur their hasty action. This couple will act as witnesses. In due time they arrive. They look to be in their fifties, a stable and intelligent man and his wife. They vouch for the man and urge me to perform the marriage ceremony. After some additional discussion between the five of us, I perform the marriage ceremony and the witnesses sign the license. The newly married couple thank me and leave. I have never heard from them since.

Another instance of a wedding which presented a dilemma: a telephone call comes from a man from Philadelphia who has been in New York for the past week. Will I marry him and his fiancee? They have their wedding license. They were at the city clerk's office early in the morning and would like to be married in the afternoon. The man apologizes for the short notice. How did he happen to call me? He says he had heard me speak at the meetings in Philadelphia over a period of years. He and his fiancee are of Protestant ancestry but are unchurched. Will I come to the Fifth Avenue Hotel and perform the wedding service? No one else is available. Will I please do him a good turn?

At four that afternoon I enter a room on an upper floor of the Fifth Avenue Hotel. There are flowers in profusion, food and drinks. The groom greets me warmly and gratefully. He is old, white-haired, and frail. He is also well educated, cultured, and apparently quite wealthy. The bride is less than half his age. There is another couple present, about the same age as the bride-to-be. They show no trace of higher education or cultural sensitivity. Both the bride and her woman friend are blondes, overdressed and excessively made up and perfumed.

We talk together. Something makes me wonder what is back of the faces and the words. Is the old man well and strong and aware of what he is doing? The bride and the two witnesses are a different kind of people from the old man. The old man seems to be secure and clear and in full possession of his faculties. Is he really making a free choice, or is he under some form of delusion? I am not entirely at ease, but I cannot think of a reason why I should refuse to be a party to what they want. I perform the ceremony. We sign the license. We drink a toast together to the happiness of the newlyweds.

Yes, I made a decision. As far as I know, I did nothing wrong. Everything was perfectly legal. They were adults and had made their decision. But I wish someone else or some others who were close to the old man had been present, friends who could have given me the sense that the marriage was in the groom's interest, in addition to his expressed desire and the obvious desire of the bride and her friends.

How should one counsel those who come to be married? Most couples do not come for advice. What of the couple where there is a pregnancy? Is that reason enough to marry?

I remember two young people, the boy twenty, the girl sixteen years old. Under the law they required parental consent and court approval. They assured me they were in love and "would have married anyway." When both mothers of the couple pleaded with me to marry them, I was persuaded to go to the Family Court to lend my support before the judge. The judge gave his approval.

Both young people were black. The families were neighbors in a public housing project on New York's West Side. The families had become friends, and both families were present in my office for the wedding. After the ceremony I was guest at the party in the housing project, a party on the grand Scale, with flowers and gay ribbons, a magnificent spread of food and drink, and one of the loudest rock bands I have ever heard. The dancing and singing lasted well into the night, with many schoolmates and friends participating. We could not hear the sounds of the city and the river and harbor—the sounds of buses, ships, truck traffic, and planes just faded out and away as if they had given up in the competition.

At Christmas the couple brought their beautiful baby to see me. The baby looked healthy and well cared for. It wore a lovely baby outfit and traveled in style in an excellent baby carriage. I felt after our visit that the young husband and wife were happy and well on the way to making a good home.

Two months later the husband phoned me. In a frantic voice he said, "Gloria has left me. I love her. The baby needs her. I'm working hard to carry my job and the home. Please get her back to me if you can."

Through her mother, I was able to reach Gloria. She was willing to come and talk with me. When I asked her whether it was true that she had left him, she said, "Sure, I left him. I should never have married so young. I never had any fun out of life. Then all of a sudden I'm tied down with a home and a baby."

I said, "When you asked me to marry you, you said you were in love. You said you would marry even if you weren't pregnant. I took you at your word. So did your families. So did the Family Court. How can you leave your husband and your child?"

Gloria looked me right in the eyes and said, 'We married because neither of us had a real home. Both families poor and without enough room for the other kids, overcrowded, noise, arguments. I didn't like school. We met after Jim finished work, and where could we meet alone? I needed love. We met in doorways. I wasn't ready for taking care of a baby, cleaning, diapers, feeding, cooking, and always waiting for Jim to come home. I wanted some fun. So I took off my wedding ring and went out dancing. His mother took care of the baby."

"Do you really want your mother-in-law to bring up your child? And haven't you any love for Jim? What's happened to you?"

She stood up. "I just can't do it. I can't stand the drudgery and the waiting and being alone. I didn't know what I was doing. I'm not going back."

This happened some years ago. Since then I have asked others and myself, was I unwise and wrong? Could I have refused to marry two young people who thought they were in love, especially when I knew they had been starved of almost everything that matters? Whatever the answer, I still have a hard time looking the judge of the Family Court straight in the eye.

A Problem Wedding

The young lady had a large witchlike hat which covered not only her hair but also her face. "Would you mind very much removing your hat?" I asked. "If I am to marry you, I really should know what you look like." Without a nod or a word, she removed her hat and revealed a very comely head and face.

They had met during the summer in Europe. He was a graduate student from Holland, she a New Yorker, still at college. Since her mother was ill, her grandmother had phoned to ask if I would marry them before their return to Europe, where they planned to live. Normally, young people do their own phoning and make their own arrangements without the help of parents or grandparents. But in this case the young man was from abroad and did not know his way around New York. There seemed to be extenuating circumstances.

In our discussion in my office the young man did most of the talking. He was lively and interesting and seemed to be very much in command of what he was doing. Among other matters, he spoke for the young woman and himself about the planning and details of the wedding, he asked how to obtain the necessary marriage license, answered intelligently questions about the attitudes of his family in Holland and possible problems of adjustment there.

The wedding was to take place in the anteroom of a small restaurant before the arrival of the noontime patrons. At the appointed time the mother and grandmother and elderly relatives of the bride were present, along with the bride, groom, and a best man and maid of honor. As we stood for the ceremony, I noticed that the groom was unusually pale. As I began to express our joy in the marriage of two young people who had found one another and loved one another and were about to join their lives across the boundaries of nations and ways of life, the young man began to grow more pale; he was having trouble keeping his eyes open, and he swayed slightly. I remember thinking that perhaps he had been up all night at a party. Perhaps he was feeling after-effects. I tried to continue the ceremony, hoping that he would recover his stability and overcome whatever was bothering him. But he grew worse. He swayed dangerously, and then his legs began to buckle. If not for the helpful support of his best man and bride, surely he would have collapsed. I took his arm and, with the help of the best man, led him to a chair. He sat down in a sort of semiconscious condition and put his head down on his knees.

Throughout this, no one said a word. The air was heavy with a dignified silence. When he seemed somewhat recovered and indicated that we might continue the ceremony, we reassembled and stood together. But again as I spoke, he swayed and seemed about to collapse. I said, "Do you take this woman to be your wife?" He nodded. The bride said, "I do." Then, with all possible haste, we led the young husband to a chair. Someone brought smelling salts.

Then conversation broke the silence. Champagne and assorted hors d'oeuvres were served. There were toasts and laughter. But the strained atmosphere remained. After I had been reassured by the mother and grandmother of the bride that all would be well, I departed.

They sailed for Holland the next morning. I have never heard a word from them since. Was it drugs? Was he tired? Or was it that he was so far from Holland and his family? I have wondered. Should I have signed the license as I did?

One Wedding Not Performed

Here is still another example of a dilemma: a program coordinator for the Johnny Carson television show phoned one day to ask if I would perform the wedding ceremony for a well-known popular TV performer, two days later. As inducement, he said that if I would perform the ceremony on the Carson Show, millions of viewers who would be watching would know for the first time that there was such a movement as Ethical Culture and Humanism. I said I would have to meet the couple to discuss the kind of wedding—their religious backgrounds and beliefs. The coordinator said, "There isn't time for all that." I indicated that I could not possibly marry the couple without some preliminary conference, and I expressed my regrets.

A night or two later I witnessed the wedding on TV. The couple were Tiny Tim and his bride. As I remember it and as I thought of it at the time, it was a caricature of a wedding, an extreme example of the exploitation of an event for the purposes of "show business."

The wedding ceremony, a celebration of love and marriage, can be exploited and distorted by parents and family, by and for market values in the community, and by the young people themselves.

For parents, the wedding of a daughter or son can be one of the happiest points in their life, a day of fulfillment of dreams for a beloved child. It can also be an occasion for parents to make clear to relatives and the community their material success, a day for establishing their social status. It can be an event to be used for business and professional or political purposes. When such motives enter into the planning of the wedding, extravagance and conspicuous consumption become part of a huge display of selecting the most prestigious place, the most elaborate decor, a lavish display of food and drink and entertainment. It may even be difficult for the guests to find the bride and groom or see them during the ceremony. Furthermore, the other family, who are partners in the marriage as parents of their son or daughter,-may be no more comfortable in such a wedding atmosphere than the young people themselves. In any case, the distortion of values makes it difficult, if not impossible, to have a shared experience of simplicity and sincerity in keeping with love and the commitment of marriage.

Just as the older generation may make it impossible for the wedding to have any spiritual quality, so the young people themselves, too, may use the wedding for purposes other than their love and marriage. It can be an occasion for the opposite extremes—a protest against formality by excessive informality, a mockery of traditional forms. In place of quiet, extreme noise; in place of privacy with families and friends, the choice of a public place, a public park, a public beach, or a stunt wedding on horseback or in an airplane to attract attention and maximum publicity.

Naturally, the public-relations and advertising industries, hotels and wedding-supply enterprises have an interest in this vast business of weddings and other ceremonies. Many tend to make them into performances, commercials, and "show business."

Most men and women planning marriage are not misled. Nor do they yield to the pressures of parents and the profit-makers when they come to discuss the event. The wedding day is still a golden day to be used for their love and their future life together and the sharing of a beautiful and memorable experience with those who are part of their personal human world.

From the Letter of a Bride

"I have no recollection of any words you spoke at my wedding. Because the marriage has not continued, I have spent a lot of time looking back to try to fathom why.

"What can I say about it? It is an occasion I recall with a complex of feelings comprised of sadness, embarrassment, and profound wonder that it ever took place. I have a blurred impression of warm lights, a confusion of voices, unknown faces. . . .

"I was happy. I was glad to be getting married. In those days I think people got married more as a matter of course than they do now. My parents encouraged it. I was only nineteen. Since Philip and I were in love and since I didn't see any reason not to get married, we proceeded along the prescribed path of preparation. As I see it now, it was in many ways my mother's wedding. The choice of you was hers—Ethical Culture was the closest affiliation any of us had with anything like a church. With most of the wedding decisions, Philip and I shrugged and acquiesced. As for the food, flowers, music, invitations—they were presented for our consideration, and we were interested but not really involved. They didn't seem relevant to the central point of being married. We took the most interest in the ring, a shopping trip we undertook on our own.

"I was quite aware of the solemnity and importance of the step in a general way, but what I didn't understand was the effort required or what it meant in terms of daily living, the give and take. Unfortunately I never learned to live that with Philip. . . .

"It pleased me to have the wedding in the house where I grew up—it is, I still think, right and fitting that ceremonies take place in familiar surroundings.

"My knowledge of weddings was from books and movies. It was comfortable to do what I believed everyone else did. So much of my way of life was like that, conforming to patterns that required no thinking or questioning. It was much later that I realized that form has no substance or meaning by itself and that content is not learned from books. So I had a sense of momentousness but no sense of my own life in relation to the occasion. I did not hear your words because in a sense I was not there—or if I was there, I was a. small divided self, distant and detached, an observer, an actress in my first big part. ...

"I remember I kept thinking, 'I am dressing for my wedding.' I didn't see Philip all day, even though he was staying in the house. It was in keeping with an old tradition, the reason for which I have no idea—an example of the meaninglessness of an empty formality. . . . I must have crossed the room with my father, but I do not remember that either. Nor what was said. I have an image of Philip's face, but I am not sure whether that's a real picture after all. I do remember turning and seeing my cousin's face all wet with tears, and I was thrilled at her emotion. ...

"I had a nice time at the wedding, but I can't recall one conversation or encounter. I smiled a lot. I know I felt interrupted when we were led to cut the cake. We were told we had to do it so the caterer could go home. It seemed a silly thing to me, and I felt foolish, but it didn't occur to me to resist or object. . . . My mother hustled us to change our clothes and leave the house. I didn't want to go so soon, but again there seemed no choice. I was a marionette on a string, and so off we went, abruptly ejected from what, according to the photographs, developed into a nice party.

"I was left with a lingering feeling that it had happened too quickly. That I had been rushed through something that I had been unable to comprehend . . . some essential core was lacking. . . ."

Solving a Human Problem

During the latter part of World War II, a worker at the USO phoned to ask if I would help a couple in trouble. A young man in uniform had fallen in love with a girl from South America. Now that the war was almost over and he was on leave, he wanted to be married. They were both devout Catholics, but they could not be married in New York City by the Church without a delay which would eat up his furlough and leave them very little or no time for a married life. They would not travel together as man and wife unless they were married. Would I perform a marriage ceremony? For them it would be a real service, but the real religious wedding would come later. Once they arrived at the bride's home, they would be welcomed by her family and probably married again in the cathedral.

I felt that the human thing to do was to marry them. I did not mind being used for their purposes, knowing that the union would lead eventually to a religious family life. Indeed, it seemed to me good that a Humanist faith could be used to serve the human situation when the Catholic requirements presented theological and legal difficulties.

Was this a mistake in judgment from the Humanist viewpoint? Was it a disservice to Catholicism?

Marriage Questions

When I began teaching, I had the illusion that I could keep children interested, all of them, all of the time. I soon found out otherwise. Similarly, when I began to perform marriage ceremonies, I had the illusion that young people that I married would stay together and would not think of separation or divorce. Although I have not kept statistics, I think the record has been unusually high for successful marriages, not only workable but happy.

A man and woman in love may be impatient with any attempt to state some minimum requirements for happiness in marriage or for a marriage to "work." We all know examples where it seems that "love conquers all." But if we look carefully, we see that love overcomes difficulties because it has in its favor a certain minimum percentage of favoring factors and conditions.

Regardless of the special adjustments required in marriages which are interfaith, interracial, or cross the lines of class, nationality, and politics, if the necessary factors are present, marriage can be happy, workable, and tolerable; without them it can be intolerable and a miserable failure. On the basis of many pre-wedding conferences and observations, I have listed some of the questions, factors, and conditions that seem to play an important part in the success or failure of a marriage.

1. Are the man and woman in love with and loving of each other? Are they ready to make commitment to each other to share, and to care for each other as husband and wife?

2. Are they coming to each other for positive, affirmative reasons? Or are they solving some other problems: marrying to escape loneliness or an impossible home situation? Marrying for romance and external attraction and sexual desire? Marrying for financial gain or more comforts or social prestige? Are they marrying in revolt against the values or authority of parents?

3. Do they have a true conviction about equality and partnership in the marriage?

4. Do they have common interests which they can share, and separate interests which they can also share and which may enrich their lives?

5. Do they have enough emotional strength and stability to make the necessary adjustments to the differences between them and the difficulties they will have to face—of illness or incapacity or in-laws, the needs and demands of children, and the hazards of the world?

6. Do they have a basic agreement on the values and priorities in life?

7. In their families and in the community immediately available to them, are there enough specific objective conditions favorable to the success of the marriage?

The First Divorce

I still remember how shocked I was when one day a young man I had married some five years before met me and told me that he and his wife had parted. When I expressed surprise and told him I had thought they were the two best-matched people I had known, he said, "We were in love when we were very young. We grew up together in school. We were well mated in every way but one. That was politics. After a few years of married life, we both became involved in party politics. We were so involved and intense about it that we ended up joining different party factions. Our meetings never came at the same time. When I was free, she was busy. When she was free, I was busy. But it was more than that. We lined up on different sides of the same issues. We began to develop different political beliefs and programs. Our political differences affected our personal relations. We began to argue, and the arguments became heated. At a certain point, whatever love we had went out of our relationship. It was not a marriage any more."

As I thought about it afterward, I had to admit that I had not considered that political ideologies or political parties could wreck a marriage. I had thought I understood how differences of religious belief and practice, and racial and national and cultural differences could make for misunderstanding and conflict. I even thought I had some insight into what class differences might do to a marriage. But here was something else, something intense and uncompromising. But why had each chosen such different ideas and alignments? Was it differences of personality and temperament that had led them to these political poles in the first place? And how could one have known ahead of time? Admittedly the weakening of affection and love could be due to personality and temperamental differences, or it could be due to pressures and divisive conflicts in the community which could bring about conditions making it difficult for a marriage to survive. If we could separate the personal factors and the social factors, could we be wiser in our choices and our counseling of those about to marry?

False Expectations

"I'll explain our problem," said the husband after two years. "We don't have any trouble about religion. We don't have any problem with our in-laws. But Maria won't give up her dancing. I love her, but I assumed that when the baby came she would stay home, give up her career and make a home. Instead of that she goes right on dancing in shows and nightclubs. It means rehearsals, late hours, going on the road, spending time with other men. I come home, and she's not there. The baby is taken care of by her mother. I didn't marry and have a child for my mother-in-law to mother. I expect to find my wife home when I finish my work. If we're going to have a marriage and a home and a family, she can't work while the baby is young."

I turned to Maria. She was blazing angry. "We never discussed or agreed that I would give up dancing," she said. "I believe it's .perfectly possible to have a career in the arts and have a marriage and a family. I had no idea that Hank would be so old-fashioned and demanding. My mother is just as good at raising our child as I am, and probably better. The child is loved and cared for better than most. I have no worry about it. But there's something more important. When I married Hank, I assumed he was not only an artist and a musician but a crack pianist, and that he might someday be a concert virtuoso. The trouble isn't my career. It's his. He hasn't worked hard enough. He isn't that good. I thought he had talent, exceptional talent. Maybe he hasn't got it. I don't know. When I met him he was a pianist in a nightclub, one of the best, and he was great. But now he gives up. He's decided that he'll do better in business. So he wants to take courses in business administration. He even wants a job with my father. I can't see it. I would never have married him if I thought that he'd work for my father. I married an artist. He turns out to be hoping to be a businessman. Believe me, it doesn't excite me at all."

Do you see what I mean? We worry about the wrong things—like religious differences. An intermarriage can make for a beautiful marriage, but it may be weakened or destroyed if it means living in a country which is strange to one of the partners and in communities where styles of life are extremely different from those back home.

An American girl of an upper-class family and Episcopal religious upbringing married a brilliant and attractive surgeon from India. The

wedding was attended by a colorful assemblage of people represent-
ing the families and relatives from India and America and many
friends from the international community of the missions to the
United Nations. No wedding could have augured more of peace in
the world and peace between man and wife. The marriage was short-
lived. Was the bride too young for her husband? Was she too young,
or too American and Western in her orientation? Was she too rigid to
adjust to Indian culture and ways of life? Was it the Indian and
Hindu rigidity? Perhaps it was all of those.

Was It a Good Marriage?

Was it a good marriage? I asked.
What do you mean by a good marriage?
    she countered.
Were you happy? Was it a happy marriage?
Was it companionable or just workable?
Was it tolerable or intolerable?
She looked at me and looked away.
I guess you could say it was happy—in the
    beginning.
But after a while he didn't really know me.
He didn't know the color of my feelings,
The cold deadness of my heart,

My moments of bitterness and despair.
We ate and slept about the same time in the same
place,
But we weren't living together.
It got to be so that whether he lived or died,
I just put him out of my mind.

Intermarriages

Many of those who come to be married have no religious affiliations or beliefs. Many come crossing the lines of religion and nationality and race. The increasing number of these intermarriages is the result of many causes, especially the growing freedom and equality of our times. People who were formerly isolated and separated from groups different from their own are now brought together by new patterns of employment, education, recreation, and travel. They have reached across the barriers of prejudice and distrust and hostility. They have discovered the common human qualities in the other human being, despite the differences; sometimes the differences are the magnetism that draws them together. Love born of different religious backgrounds, races, colors, and nationalities can be exciting and irresistible. It may also be blind to the realities and strong in its determination not to be denied. Two religious sects can be in conflict, two nations may be at war, two languages and cultural patterns may make communication difficult—like the combination of Zulu and Greek described earlier—and yet young people meet and love and marry. They may do so in the face of parental opposition and community resentment and rejection.

In cases of interfaith marriage, the couple often seeks a compromise as a solution for their conflicting religious affiliations and beliefs. They may come to the Ethical Culture Society because of the: objections or pressures of prospective in-laws or their own parents. Or they come seeking a common ground and a new basis for a marriage and family life. Others come to find a positive answer for themselves in their marriage, and for the children they hope to bring into the world. They look forward to a child, wanting him to know his ancestry, but also wanting him to have an identity with an inclusive human community which stands for an affirmative philosophy and faith.

Sometimes the marriage of two people from similar religious backgrounds, whether Catholic or Protestant or Jewish, who differ greatly in the intensity of their faiths can pose problems more serious than those met in an intermarriage. Two young Protestants once sat in my office, the man explaining that he was "way out of the fold, practically an atheist," while the woman was a strict Presbyterian. The man said that his knowledge of the philosophy of the Ethical Movement had convinced him that this was the only place where he could be married with any integrity. Although his fiancee was uncertain, she indicated she could accept an Ethical service. I asked whether diat meant that she was willing to compromise on the wedding for the sake of the marriage. She said yes. 1 pointed out that, while the wedding was not as important as the marriage, if it put her in the position of compromising on basic beliefs, she could have real trouble afterward. Unless both were really in accord in their basic philosophy and faith, the compromise on the wedding could mislead them into a marriage beset with serious religious problems, such as church attendance, contributions, the celebration of religious holidays. Even more serious might be conflict over how they would bring up their children, what they would do about baptism or confirmation and religious upbringing, and relationships with in-laws.

They insisted that their love was real, and that they wished to share life together. I suggested that some differences can be worked out, but that there should be no major difference in purpose and basic beliefs: their opposing religious beliefs could cause havoc. I suggested that they think it over and talk it out before agreeing to a compromise wedding which could please only because it did not offend. They left, postponing their decisions—and I never saw them again.

Many of the religious intermarriages work out well if the partners have the basic understandings that make any good marriage. It is important that they come to the intermarriage for positive reasons: not to escape, not to punish their parents, not to overcompensate out of compassion for someone from a minority group or another faith, not to run away from something in their past or their family. They must come to the marriage out of mutual love and strength, not out of weakness.

One of the stumbling blocks for interfaith couples has been the tradition of each religious sect that it alone has the absolute truth and revelation, and that it must preserve itself from contamination by outside beliefs. The ecumenical movement has begun to recognize and respect the sincerity and value of different religions, but what is back of the talk of unity? Is monotheism the bridge and base for communication between people of differing religious sects? Ecumenicism has meant that priests, rabbis, and ministers respect each other as religious leaders. They agree to avoid being intolerant. They agree to cooperate on common objectives. They will speak in each other's pulpits. They can surely cooperate in common concerns just as long as they do not try to force unity in the basic religious differences.

A year or two after World War II, a couple asked me to conduct their wedding service. She was a teacher in the public schools, of Protestant ancestry; he was an engineer, of Italian birth and Catholic background, but now an atheist. In our discussion of the wedding he said, "I am well satisfied with Ethical Humanism as a philosophy and a good basis for our life together. But I have one problem: my mother has spent most of her life in Italy. Now she is old and a devout and observing member of the Church. She just wouldn't understand if her only son was to be married without a priest being present. Could a priest be present at the wedding and say a prayer or a blessing?"

I told him it might be difficult to find a priest who would be willing and who was not restricted by the Church. I said I would ask a friend, the most liberal priest I knew, a man with a warm heart. We had worked on many social problems together.

I telephoned him. As usual, he greeted me most heartily. But as I described the problem of the young man and his mother, I could sense the temperature going down at the other end of the phone. The priest finally said, "Al, I would do anything you ask, anything I can do, but we have rules. I can't do it. This is governed by the disciplines of the Church. I hope you will understand."

"Would you see the couple?" I asked. "It would mean a lot to them to talk with you. Perhaps you can help them."

"Of course I'll talk with them," he answered.

They went to see him. He arranged to marry them.

Many clergymen have united in coalitions on delinquency and housing for the poor, the rights of conscientious objectors, opposition to the war in Vietnam, voter registration, and a boycott of non-union lettuce from the West. But there are basic areas where they cannot see eye to eye. ∎.

The mother of a young woman came to see me. Her daughter was of Jewish ancestry. The son-in-law-to-be was Catholic. Did I know a priest and a rabbi who would be willing to cooperate in a joint wedding service? The only priest available in this instance was a young Jesuit working with poor people, and the rabbi was a long-time friend. The scarcity of clergy able to cooperate on joint ceremonies is understandable: how can they cooperate if it means a compromise of their basic religious assumptions?

"Is This a Marriage?"

Another marriage I remember was between a Catholic and a Protestant. The ceremony was held in a hotel on lower Fifth Avenue, with about sixty guests, family and friends. At the point where the groom and the bride made their commitments, saying, "With this ring I thee wed," the mother of the bride rose, waving her arms hysterically. She cried out, "Is this a marriage? This is no marriage. This is no marriage!" I ended the ceremony as quickly as possible. The bride and the groom kissed each other, and the guests gathered around to congratulate them and embrace them. But the mother walked away. I followed her, took her arm, and led her to a corner of the room. "You love your daughter," I said. "I know you do. You've been a good mother; it shows in the kind of daughter you have. She will lead a good life. She will make a good home and family: Don't you want her to be happy? Even if you disagree with what she is doing, you have to give her your good will, your support, your blessing. If not, why did you come? Why do you want to destroy her with unhappiness on this most important day of her life?"

She glowered at me; nothing would quiet her. It was the quiet strength of the young couple, and the warm affection and solidarity of support of their many friends, that healed the hurt to some extent—never completely, I am sure. But when the wedding party was over, it; seemed to me that the reality of the love of these two young people, would live on, despite the differences of religion. What they were, what they brought to their marriage, was a common ground on which they could build a life.

The Broken Glass

In Judaism an important symbolism in the wedding ceremony is the glass of wine and the breaking of the glass. The wine is blessed by the rabbi. He holds the glass to the groom's lips, and then he or the groom holds the glass to the bride's lips so that she too may drink. When each has partaken of the wine, the groom places the glass under his heel and breaks it.

There are diverse explanations for this act. One holds that it symbolizes the breaking of the hymen; another, that no one shall drink from the same glass to which husband and wife have touched their lips. The traditional religious meaning is that even in the midst of joy, one should remember that sorrow, too, is part of life; that one should remember the destruction of the Temple in Jerusalem, that just as the glass is shattered and the fragments scattered, so the scattered remnants of the Jewish people must remember their unity, their common heritage, and the promise of reunion in Israel.

After one wedding, at which the ceremony was in the Humanist tradition, the young husband and wife led their families and guests out on the roof terrace, open to the sun and blue sky. Tables had been set with food and wine. As the wedding party took their seats a strong breeze shook the tables and lifted one of the table coverings. As a glass fell and broke, one of the relatives clapped her hands with joy. "Now," she exclaimed joyously,. "it's a Jewish wedding after all!"

An Arab-Israeli Intermarriage

In the aftermath of the Arab-Israeli War of 1948—1949, a woman of Arab background and a man of Jewish ancestry asked to be married at the Ethical Culture Society. Music had brought them together. She was a singer and he a member of the orchestra, both with the Metropolitan Opera Company. Despite the centuries of fear and conflict in their backgrounds, they said they did not believe the kind of hate talk that was current. "We have never accepted that kind of nonsense," said the man. The woman said, "Most people say that when people of different backgrounds come together, it's despite the differences. With us it's the opposite: we find our differences more interesting and exciting, and we are more attracted by our differences than by the things we have in common." He added, "When people know each other the way we do, it's impossible to hate."

Because their families did not share their views, they were married secretly. I conducted the wedding in my office with two Ethical Society staff members as witnesses. The "service" was in the nature of a sitting-down discussion.

To officiate at their wedding was a double pleasure for me. The bride and groom were wonderful people, extremely sensitive to beauty and full of zest for life, and intelligent and progressive in their hopes for the world. Perhaps I was drawn to them particularly because of my own love of music and the consciousness-expanding experiences of my teen years: the opportunity to be a super or extra at the old Met in the days of Caruso. Although we had no music in my office during the wedding, I know that there was music all around us and inside us as we looked into each other's faces and talked—the music of the magic world of Verdi, Bizet, Puccini, Wagner, Donizetti, Rimsky-Korsakoff. When it came time to say a public and legal "I do," we stood up together. The bride and groom each made a commitment to the other, exchanged rings, and sealed it with a kiss.

Within a year their two families were curious and possibly had sensed the importance of the relationship. The marriage was then made known to them. To everyone's relief and joy, the marriage was accepted and became a source of happiness to all concerned. They have since had the happiest of marriages. Love and music have graced the lives of their lovely children, their families, and their friends and their many associates in the world of music.

In the years since the wedding, whenever I have addressed the Ethical Societies in New Jersey and Long Island, or the Annual Assembly of the American Ethical Union, the wife, Virginia, often makes it a point to be there and to add her lovely voice, usually with an aria from an opera—"Vissi d'Arte" from *Tosca,* and others. Yes, she sings for all those present, and for me, and I love it. And when she does, the memory of the voices of Bori, Matzenauer, Farrar, Amato, Ponselle, comes back to me—and it brings back the wedding.

The couple had indicated that for them it was a "love of life" and a "love for life." At the end I had quoted Conrad Aiken: "Music I heard with you was more than music. And bread I broke with you was more than bread." May it always be so for them!

Another happy marriage took place when a young American, a Protestant from New York City, returned from a tour of service with the Peace Corps in Thailand. He had fallen in love with the land, the culture, the way of life, and the people of Thailand—in particular, Tuenchai. Tuenchai, a nurse, came with him to the United States to be married. At the wedding in the Meeting House of the Ethical Society, the bride, beautiful and shy, was attended by at least a half-dozen Thai girls, all of whom were nurses. They were dressed in similar native Thai dresses. Their quiet and simplicity and the beauty of their persons as well as their dress made for a mood which is hard to describe. They were all part of something very lovely.

Here was a wedding which united two lovely and loving people across the lines of nationalism—not to mention difference of religious tradition and diverse cultural ways of life.

Years ago, Eleanor Roosevelt said, "Beyond whatever good the Peace Corps may do for underdeveloped nations and relations between the United States and other nations, this country will benefit internally by the education of those who are part of the Peace Corps and return to the States better able to understand people and problems and contribute to better life here at home." I think she forgot to mention the many marriages that also came out of the experience.

In an Old Dutch Reform Church

The place they selected for their wedding was a little old Dutch church with ivy-covered walls nestling against a hillside, commanding a grand view of the Hudson River Valley at Spuyten Duyvil, where the Harlem and Hudson Rivers join their waters.

The bride and groom had met while working in a famous nightclub. Both were young, attractive, and talented; she was a dancer, he a pianist with the band. She was of Spanish and Catholic ancestry, he American and Jewish. The Spanish family were liberal, rationalists and atheists. The Jewish relatives identified with Reform Judaism.

Before the wedding ceremony the families and friends gathered outside the church to greet each other and enjoy the midsummer sun and the beautiful vistas of the Hudson. If either family had any reservations about the marriage, they gave no evidence of it. Each family acted with dignity and friendliness. No doubt each was proud—the parents of the bride aware of their daughter's beauty and talents and independence of spirit, the parents of the groom gratified by their son's accomplishments and loving him. Both families joined the gaiety of the young people, who were fellow workers and fellow artists from the nightclub. These were interesting and beautiful young people, dancers, singers, comedians, members of the band and management. Even before they entered the church, the mood of the assemblage reflected the emotion and sentimentality of those whose lives are bound to the precarious world of theaters, nightclubs, and the entertainment industry. The common devotion to the arts, the insecurity of a highly competitive occupation, and their respect for one another's talents—these made for affection and solidarity. Differences of religion and race did not matter.

Parental Attitudes

A letter came in the mail from a woman unknown to me.

" . . . I am turning to you with a desperate heart. I have just learned that my son plans to marry a black girl.

"My son has just left college (a graduate student). He has not given himself an opportunity to explore life. He hasn't traveled or sown wild oats or just gone out with other women.

"He has left us bereft. He is doing it all for the wrong reasons. Perhaps you will label me white middle-class. But we cannot identify and relate to black in-laws. We have to be honest about this. We would love anybody our son loves. We would relate to any family he joins in marriage and family life. But the culture and traditions of black people are so completely different from our own. And how can they relate to us?

"The painful thing is that the relationship has gone on for some time in secret. It leaves us sick and bewildered. Will you meet with our son and help him see the problems of an interracial marriage, the misery he is letting himself in for? Please!"

This was my reply to the mother:

"The real question is whether your son and the girl he is in love with have the elements that will make a good marriage. If they really love one another and if they have interests which they share and which will make life interesting and if they are both fairly well-adjusted people who can live through difficult days as well as the easy happy ones, if they have the same sense of values in life, then they can have a happy marriage—and I am sure that that's what you want most for your son, happiness.

"It is true that an interracial marriage has certain special difficulties. There are certain parts of the country where they will not be able to live. There will be some people even in such a liberal place as New York who will be critical. It will be difficult for the children. But despite all these difficulties, if they have strength and true love they will be able to work their problems out together.

"If you knew that your son were going off to war or if your son had some fatal disease, you would see this thing differently. You would want him to have whatever happiness he can have while he still lives. If he chose a girl who was white and Jewish but still was a girl who would hurt him or waste his life, I am sure you would feel far worse than if he marries a girl whose skin is brown but who has beauty and character and talent and who loves your son. I am sure that this is very difficult for you to understand and to adjust to. If you are opposed to his marriage, you surely have the right and obligation to state your opposition, your arguments, your feelings about the difficulties of an interracial marriage. I think you should state these openly and honestly to your son but do this with control of your feelings so that he has no reason to become angry with you or alienated or to feel that you do not love him.

"If after you have expressed your opposition he still insists on marrying her, I hope that you will give him and her a feeling of support and help them in every way you can. You may find that this will be a very wonderful marriage and that good things may come of it. It is also possible that the marriage may have difficulties and that it may fall apart, either because they are not really suited to one another or because the pressures of the community are too great for them to bear. In the time in which we live, a certain number of young people will have to try things out and learn from their mistakes. This need not be a tragedy, and it is not inevitable that evil should come of it.

"If your son, after talking with you, would like to make a date with me, I would be very glad to see him and the young lady. I hope that, whatever happens, you will not lose touch with your son. I wish you all the best."

She never acknowledged my letter or called me.

My Worst Enemy

The following words were actually said by a father to
his daughter's 'prospective husband years ago. I
arranged them in this form in an effort to catch the
quality of his intensity.

"Sure, I want my daughter to marry,
And you're a fine young man,
But you're the last man I'd want her to marry.
Because of you my whole world is ruined.
Where I've worked twenty-five years
I can't tell them.
They'd feel sorry for me.
I'll have to sell my house.
I'm finished in the neighborhood.
I can't give the same wedding I gave my other
daughter.
I can't tell my mother or my wife's mother.
I can't even put your picture on the piano.
It's as if you walked past me
And by walking you made a draft.
From this draft I caught a cold,
From the cold I got pneumonia,
And from this I died.
You see what I mean?

You've killed me.
You may be a fine young man
But you're my worst enemy."

Interracial Marriages

Interracial marriages have the same problems as all other marriages. In addition, they may suffer or benefit from the special challenges of family opposition and the resistance and pressures of many communities. Although racial mixture has been part of the life of the human race in many parts of the world for a long time, it has been outlawed by state laws in many parts of the United States. And although the Supreme Court declared such laws unconstitutional in 1967, interracial marriages still suffer from community rejection and punitive practices and deprivations.

In part this is because of the history of slavery in the United States, and the effect of the Civil War and the experience and aftermath of the postwar period of Reconstruction. These have left their mark on black and white people,-especially in their prejudices and distrust and ignorance of each other. And insofar as black .people have generally suffered deprivation, discrimination, and segregation, the difference of color is not merely a matter of color. It is a matter of class distinctions and a pattern of different ways of life.

When I say that interracial marriages may suffer or benefit from the challenges of opposition, I mean that for some couples the resistance to their desire to make a life together may destroy their chances, while for other couples the very factors which present difficulty will bring out their strength and love and will to make a home and family and fulfill their love.

The question is, do they understand the basic conditions which make possible a marriage? And what are the needs and desires which drew them together in the first place? Despite the traditional attitudes and laws and customs and practices against intermarriage, the number of such marriages has been on the increase in recent years. And these intermarriages are not on the fringes of conventional society: they are-evident in increasing numbers among the middle class and the educated and the most cultivated as well as up and down all income levels. More and more people recognize that the white prejudice which rejected black people as inferior in basic nature and potentialities is a contradiction of scientific findings. And increasing numbers are now aware that the prejudice against people of Asian as well as African ancestry, against people with different-colored skins, yellow, and brown and black, is a sign of ignorance and conditioning. And indoctrination from the past. It cannot be a part of the attitude and practice of civilized human beings.

An interracial marriage can be the source of a richer life for both partners, a truly happy and creative husband-and-wife relationship, and may produce children of unusual beauty and gifts. Such marriages can do a great deal for members of the two families of origin, and also for the education and enrichment of the community. But also they can fail, and when they do there is possibly more misery than in separation and divorce between two people from the same background, because there may be a tendency to blame the inadequacies of each on the racial factor, and to fall back on stereotypes in criticizing each other.

Where frictions develop, counseling may be of help. Therapy, on the other hand, may bring to the surface hidden aspects of the personality and reveal that the marriage was a mistake. The placid, gentle, compassionate person may become aggressive and openly resentful and critical, and demand adjustments rather than make them.

Much of the difficulty of interracial marriages would be obviated, and the benefits of interracial marriages enjoyed, if more children and youth were taught to respect all' people and all differences, and to reach out to their fellow men, and to strive for understanding of their neighbors. The more we rid ourselves of prejudices, stereotypes, and scapegoats in our thinking about "groups" other than "our own," the more we can create a climate in which people communicate,, trust, know, and enjoy one another. Out of the rich mixture and interplay of differences can come a better and richer life for all of us.

If we succeed, the concept of "half-breed" as a mark of inferiority will fade out of the human mind and heart: Then mixed marriages will enjoy acceptance and support from the community. Men and women of different racial backgrounds will be able to work out their' marriages under material, psychological, social, and spiritual conditions that give support to all that is best in marriage and family life as part of a truly democratic culture.

Interracial Divorce

A father called one day. He was a teacher and head of his department at a high school in the city.. He said, "My daughter, Dorothy, wants to be married, and she wants you to marry her. You know her. The young man is Negro. This young man is highly intelligent and attractive and no doubt will have a very distinguished career in medicine. He is a good student and has been admitted to one of the good medical schools. My wife and I think our daughter may not be ready for marriage and certainly not ready for the complications of this marriage. A marriage like this might work out all right in Paris or Latin America or the Caribbean countries. We doubt it can work out in the United States with any real happiness. I have urged my daughter to talk it out with someone outside the family. She and the young man should have some help in facing what they are going to be up against. They've got to face some of the realities they'll have to live with. I'm calling because I have pressed them on this matter. They may be ready to talk with you. Will you see them?"

"I'll be glad to see them and talk with them. But I want to be very straight with you. I will try to help them face the problems they might face. I will not try to dissuade them from marrying. If they are well matched and love each other, if they are marrying one another for sound reasons, and if they have most of the conditions and the elements that make a good marriage, then they and they alone must decide."

"If you will do that, I will accept what comes," said the father.

The couple called and made an appointment. She was white, blond, a former student of mine, now a teacher in the public schools. The young man was black, handsome, talented, bright, and charming. I felt I could understand their attraction and their love for each other.

After the greetings and introduction of her fiance, Dorothy said, "We really don't see any point in talking. We love each other and we want to be married. We're doing this to please my father. I respect my parents. My father is upset. He has always been a wonderful example of a liberal, democratic human being. I honestly don't think you could find a more liberal person anywhere. I think he's afraid for me. It's part of his love for me. He's overprotective. I'm grown up enough to take care of myself. I feel very sure about this. We know what we're doing."

"I take it that we are going to be frank with each other. I have no interest in your decision other than good wishes for both of you and the desire to be helpful at this time when you are making one of the most important decisions of your life. Now, one of the questions is: Are you really in love and how do you know it? Another is: Have you been drawn to each other for the best reasons, sound needs and desires? Or could it be that in crossing the lines of religion and race, without knowing it consciously you are turning away from the world of your family or the people with whom you would normally identify? In other words, are there negative reasons more than positive reasons that make you turn toward each other despite or because of the differences between you? Or is your choice really independent of your differences—rather that you see and experience in each other the qualities which you would embrace even if you were of the same religious and racial background?

"And the last question has to do with whether or not you will have enough going for you in the external situation, enough of the elements and conditions which would make marriage likely to work and result in happiness? For if the necessary minimum of conditions is lacking or the obstacles and difficulties are too great, then you will have to have unusual love and ability and will-power and commitment to overcome them.

"In some states it is difficult and even dangerous for an interracial couple to live together. In many states and local communities where it may be safe to live, the reality includes prejudiced attitudes and discrimination in housing, employment, and schools."

"We know all that," said the young man. "I am going into medicine. I know that many hospitals will refuse to have me as an intern or resident. Many institutions will refuse me a hospital appointment even if I specialize and have special competence in a given field in medicine. Does that mean I shouldn't study to be a doctor? I know that some medical societies do not admit black doctors. I know that not only white people but even some black people will not use a black doctor."

Over two long sessions in which we discussed the marriage relationship, race relations in education and medicine, the possible problems of children of interracial marriages, and the relationship with their families, we tried to face together the attitudes and practices which might present difficulty and the trends which suggested that race relations might improve in the next few years. When we had exhausted the problems and ourselves, the couple in almost a single voice said, "And now, will you marry us?"

While they were still with me, I telephoned Dorothy's father. At the end of my report I said, "They have asked me to marry them. I hope you will go along with the marriage."

The wedding date and time were agreed upon. Both families appeared at the appointed time. All stood for the ceremony. Tears streamed down the face of the father of the bride. When the ceremony was over, the father not only kissed his daughter but he put his arms around the young husband and said, "My son."

Ten years later the young medical student, now a practicing doctor, telephoned me. He was very upset. "My wife has put me out," he said. "I'm not able to see her or enter my home or see my children. Will you make contact with her? Will you ask her to meet with me in your office so we can talk together? We haven't communicated for so long. I'm desperate."

As I remembered the bride, she had been shy and quiet and unassuming, almost painfully so. I knew she was sensitive, intelligent, and talented. What had happened to her in the ten years of the marriage? Now there were three children. How had she changed?

They came into my office. She would not speak with him. She would not look at him. I could see that she had grown a great deal in strength and capacity for expression. Her eyes spoke her resentments, bitterness, and anger. She said, "When we were married we loved one another and made our commitments to each other. I gave him everything. I taught school and supported both of us while he went to medical school. He worked hard at his studies. He lived in the hospital when he was an intern and resident. I helped him .start his practice. Now he is a successful doctor. He has his own office. He has wealthy patients. I thought he loved me. Maybe he did—when he needed me—but that passed. He hasn't been a husband to me. He hasn't treated me as an equal or with any human consideration. He has given little fatherly affection, support, or relationship to his children. I have had the full burden. He lives his own life and he comes and goes as he pleases. He practically drove me insane by his mistreatment of me—it was degrading, demeaning. I couldn't stand it. I began to hate him. I began to hate myself. I wouldn't let him touch me. I loathed him. I went into therapy to save my life. More and more I began to see what our relationship had been and what it had become and what I must do if I was *to* survive at all, and if the children were to grow up at all healthy. Our home had become a place of conflict and hurt. I'm through with therapy, and I'm through with him."

We may ask: What made the marriage fail? Was it due to the difference of color? Or was it temperament and inequality in the relationship? It might have been sexual incompatibility. It might have been the racial attitudes in the larger community. But the wife felt that possibly she had been compassionate and romantic because he was a member of a people who had suffered racial discrimination and rejection and persecution. She was romantic concerning him and the role she might play in righting racial mistreatments of the past. Now that he was strong and educated and a successful professional man making his way without her help, he no longer needed her. She had' supported him and had- tied herself down with home and children. The needs of both had changed. Now she could no longer accept her earlier role. Nor could he accept and adjust to her new role, her demand for equality and freedom and her own fulfillment.

Who is wise enough to unravel such a relationship and be positive that this was the one and only cause of the marriage failure? It is easy to place the blame on the intermarriage of men and women of different religions, nationalities, and races and classes. No doubt the intermarriage factors play a part in many failures. But more often than not the real causes lie in the normal problems of personality adjustments, the problems of living together, and community conditions which may have nothing to do with the intermarriage aspect.

Through the years I have officiated at and participated in many weddings of men and women of diverse backgrounds, religious and racial, and national: European, Asian, African, and North and South American. The marriages have crossed the lines of nationality and language and culture. They have joined men and women in love across the boundaries and' prejudices which separate the Americas, North and South and in-between, and have reached out across continents, Asian, African, and European. Those who have come to be married have sought a common ground of human values and human responsibility. They have believed in each other. They have believed in the tremendous potentialities of the human mind and heart. They have been willing and eager to stake their lives on their faith.

Our Daughter-in-Law

These lines ex-press the feelings of a mother who was close to her son and who, in her life style and relationships, expected a daughter-in-law to be close to her. The young wife came from a background where people were reserved even in family relationships and feelings were not easily and fully articulated.

From the moment of the wedding
Something was wrong.
I helped her dress, but she never said, "Thank you."
She never told me how I looked.
I bring her a plant or praise her living room,

I feed her at a restaurant or cook with my own
hands,
She never says anything.
She won't call us "Mom" and "Dad."
She says where she came from
People don't talk much and they don't express
their
feelings.
She says we swarm all over her.
She says she's against "togetherness."
Our son says we make it hard for him
He has to be loyal to her even when she's wrong.
Do you think maybe she'll accept us
When she has a baby?

"Cabin Fever"

In the country an elderly skilled craftsman submitted
a bill for work he had done. When I paid the bill by
check, I wrote a note asking how he had weathered the
winter. The following sentiments were written across
the bottom of the receipted bill.

I'm sorry you asked
About the winter.
You might say my wife and I were "frozen in."
From this we caught
The worst case of "cabin fever" you could ever imagine.
My wife and I never saw
So much of each other.
After forty years of married life
It was hard for either one
To show any new side of personality
At 30 below.
To relieve the monotony
We didn't come to blows
But it sure was a borderline case.
I'd say
The winter was almost
Murderous.

The Marriage of Two Grandparents

Two elderly friends, both widowed and both having
had very happy marriages, asked if I would conduct a
wedding service for them. Present were their grown
and married sons and daughters and the grandchildren.
This is what I said as part of the wedding ceremony.

First I will speak simply to you, the grandchildren, so that everybody will understand what is happening here and now. It is a happy time for all of us. I hope it will be a happy time for you. Usually *-parents* see the son or daughter married. Usually a grandfather and a grandmother see a grandchild married. Today it is going to be the opposite. A son and daughter are going to see a father and mother married, the grandchildren like you are going to see a grandpa and grandma married. That is unusual, and it is a lot of fun for you, as it is for them.

It is not much fun to live by yourself. Everybody needs and wants to 'be with somebody else and to find someone to live with, somebody he knows and likes, somebody he loves. We wish that everybody in the world would find somebody and like somebody and then on a certain day say, "We love each other. We want to live together. Let's make a home together."

The world has many strange things. That makes it very important that everybody should have a home, a place to come to, which is his own and her own. No matter what happens in the world: war or other trouble, cold winter or hot summer, every one of us should have a home, a place to live with somebody who warms us and whom we want to live with.

Do you know what a home is? It is a place where you are safe from the rain and snow, from the freezing cold of winter and the burning hot sun of summer. It is a place where somebody is waiting for you and wants you and where you take care of each other. Now Philip and Mary are going to have a home together. They will have good times together with many friends, and if Philip or Mary does not feel well, each will take care of the other. They will want you to come and visit and stay with them and share some good food and good times. I am sure that they love you very much.

When we get older we usually cannot run as fast as we used to. We cannot do all the things we want to do. So it is very important to .have somebody who will grow old with us, somebody who will always be nearby. Now, Philip will get older, but he will never be an old man. He will always be young. There is a lot of fun in him. And Mary is like ;that too. When they live together, they will keep each other young. One of the things that will keep them young is you. The more you are around them, the more they will be young, because there is nothing that helps older people to be young more than to have boys and girls around who love them. That is what they will want more than anything else.

Now, Philip and Mary, nobody can really marry you but your-selves. It is what you mean in your heart and the promise you make to one another. When I speak, I am speaking for you and for all of us. We believe you will love one another, take care of one another, make a beautiful home for yourselves and those who love you. We hope that you will always find peace of mind and always find joyful-ness in your home and that you will always have zest for life and look forward to tomorrow. To your last breath you will always be young and gay and happy together and share each other's life and enrich each other in every way.

Knowing both of you, we know that the love you bring to this marriage is not a blind love but a love out of seeing and knowing each other. We believe that you will have true security in one another, and that you will always have a deep faith in life because you have found one another and share one another's life.

May you always be able to express two thoughts, two convictions, to each other: Because I know the good in you, the one I love ...

Philip and Mary, will you put on the ring and say these words? "With this ring I thee wed, in love and truth, in joy and sorrow, through life."

A Remarriage
after Many Years

I had married this man and woman twenty years before. After twelve years they divorced each other. Then, after eight years, they asked me to conduct a service of remarriage.

Joseph and Anna, although we who are with you at this happy moment are few, you must know that your many friends and loved ones will rejoice when they know that you are being remarried.

The form of our ceremony should be a true expression of the meaning of the occasion. It should be personal and informal, an expression of our feeling and thought, meaningful and true for you and all of us.

Well over two thousand years ago Plato wrote the *Symposium*. The *Symposium* is a discussion of love. Socrates and his companions decided that they would discuss the meaning of love. They thought that the theme of their symposium would be best served if each in turn raised his cup of wine and proposed a toast to love. Each made his toast in a prayer or poetry or in a statement of explanation or tribute. One interpretation held that long, long ago, human beings were not divided into male and female, man and woman. They were whole beings. Then Zeus divided each being into two halves, and so they were separated into man and woman. But they knew no peace. They suffered and yearned for each other. They were drawn together as if by some magnetic force, some magic of the heart. They yearned for union with each other. It is this hunger of the whole being, this gravitation of the soul, that draws man and woman together, despite all differences and difficulties. Without this union there is no life. Without this love life loses its beauty and its goodness. For love draws together all things natural and human.

And so it is with you: whatever divided and separated you, the power of love and the desire for the wholeness of life have reunited you today in this marriage.

It has been said that no one lives to himself alone and no one dies to himself alone. We need each other. And in this time of world confusion and conflict the personal relationship is more important to us than ever. Whatever meaning life may have, the key is in our human world, in the few we treasure as friends and in the one above all others, the one in whom we find caring and being cared for, forgiving and being forgiven, loving and being loved. And it is important as we grow older.

We hope that the happiness you seek and find will be deeper than pleasure and beyond all pain; a happiness as deep and profound as anything man knows. It may be an experience of creativeness, a glimpse of beauty or of human goodness or a grasp of some understanding beyond knowledge, a deeper wisdom of life. In your lives together we hope you will have many such moments to carry you through.

You who were separated have turned back to each other. You who were apart are brought back to be reunited, to share life and love.

Some people believe that every husband and wife should be remarried at certain times when they discover and rediscover one another. For with the experiences we all go through and the ways we change and grow, it is good to know what we are doing with our lives. With this in mind:

Do you, Joseph, take this woman to be your wife?

Do you, Anna, take this man to be your husband?

Now then, on behalf of the larger community and all who love you, may I say that we rejoice that you can use again two old and dear names, husband and wife.

Out of your marriage we hope you will be reborn and regenerated and know as never before the joy of sharing and loving life.

The Heroic Spirit

Robert Frost was his name. I knew him as a boy when he attended the religious education program of the Ethical Society. His family were members. At an Air Force base in Florida, on a hot sunny afternoon during World War II, he and his fellow pilots-in-training had their wings pinned on in a formal ceremony. That night a few of the new pilots went into town to celebrate. After a long, boisterous evening, they sang exuberantly as they were being driven back to the base in their jeep at high speed. Then suddenly, out of the morning mist, a dog appeared on the dark road. The driver swerved. All were thrown out. The only one seriously injured was Bob. His spine was broken.

For a long period he was in an iron lung in Florida. Then he was sent to the Veterans' Administration Hospital in New York City. When I visited him there, he lay paralyzed, kept alive by many tubes connected to instruments. There was no self-pity; only an amazing courage and a will to live. He was deeply grateful to his Polish-born nurse. I was impressed with her competence and devotion but quite unprepared for the phone call that came from Bob some months later. He told me that he and the nurse wished to marry, and wanted me to perform the wedding ceremony. We set the date; his parents would be present.

About a week before the wedding, the nurse made an appointment to see me. Born and brought up as a devout Catholic, she wanted to talk about the religious questions, the meaning of the Humanist marriage service. She had a child by a former marriage. Bob not only loved her but planned to adopt the child. Her love for Bob was now central in her own life, but questions about the religious future of her son still had to be faced.

On the agreed date, the nurse wheeled Bob into my office. Sitting in his wheelchair, with his parents at his side, he took the nurse's hand. I said, "If anything can heal our pain and make us whole, it is love. And whatever hurt we do or suffer, we can heal ourselves and one another. So it is in the love that makes a marriage. Will you repeat after me these words: 'With this ring I thee wed, in joy and sorrow, in love and truth, through life.' "

After months more of treatment, they moved into a ground-floor apartment in a lovely housing development in Hastings-on-Hudson. Bob had a veteran's pension, but he needed to earn enough to support his family. From his wheelchair he carried on a business, manufacturing batteries, flashlights, and reflectors; he even visited the factory departments. In addition, he devoted himself to civic work—above all, work for other disabled veterans. He became a Commander of the Disabled American Veterans and a founder of Albert Einstein Medical College.

When he died some years later, citizens of Hastings, members of veterans' organizations, of the Real Estate Board, and many neighbors were present at the memorial services to pay tribute. In the face of overwhelming catastrophe he had provided for a wife and a child and a family. He had in ten brief years lived a new life as husband, father, worker, citizen, a man with a will to live and a heroic will to overcome.

Terminal Marriage

I remember marrying a young soldier who came back from the Pacific during World War II. He had been stocky and strong, an athlete. But then he developed cancer of the throat. While undergoing treatments at Walter Reed Army Hospital in Washington, D.C., he encountered a girl to whom he had been very attached in his schooldays. She was working in one of the government offices. In the crowded and exciting conditions of wartime in the nation's capital, they were drawn to each other more than ever. They fell in love and decided to marry.

When they met with me in New York to discuss their plans for the wedding, it was an unusual pre-wedding conference. The bride was beautiful, enthusiastic, and spirited. The young soldier gave evidence of the seriousness of his illness. The treatments had heen very intense and had left him weak. He could hardly speak. The girl did most of the talking. It was clear that they were very close and that she spoke for him as well as for herself. She asked if the wedding could be held on the beautiful grounds at the Fieldston School in Riverdale. She explained that his sister had once attended the Encampment for Citizenship, a citizen-training camp held there in the summertime. It would be a small wedding; only the two families would be present.

It was early in the summer, but the Encampment had already begun. I was living and working there. It was easy to arrange. We agreed on a day when the campers would be off on a field trip. On the wedding day, two cars drove up to the school, as close as they could get to the administration building. I was waiting for them. The bride and groom and the two families walked slowly up through the grass and up the steps to the office of the principal. The few steps were difficult for the groom, but the principal's office had spacious windows extending the entire length of the east wall of the room and gave out on the lush foliage of the school grounds in the late-afternoon sun. As we stood together in silence for a few moments, I looked into the faces of the parents and then of the bride and the groom. Everyone was quite aware of the seriousness of the ailment and the possibility that this marriage might not last long. I could not speak with lightheartedness or gaiety, nor could I give in to my sense of tragedy. I spoke of what human beings have meant by the great love that can be between a man and a woman. I spoke of the courage that makes that love possible, and the generous giving and the mutuality that makes for fulfillment. And the understanding that true happiness is much deeper than pleasure and transcends pain. When I asked the groom, "Do you take this woman to be your wife?" his voice was barely audible as he said, "I do." Her answer, too, was quiet, but there was a light in her eyes that seemed to me to be able to sustain anything. There was no question but they were both in love. They kissed each other, they were embraced by their families, and the two families departed with the young couple to have dinner together.

Two years later, I was called to conduct the funeral service. Before I walked into the room where the service was to be held, I took the young wife aside. We talked about their life together. How had it been with her? She answered me very simply. It had been difficult and at times agonizing. But her eyes glowed with love as she said, "It was a tremendous experience for both of us. I wouldn't have given it up for anything. We shared many happinesses. I have absolutely no regrets. I would do it all over again, if only I could. It was a good marriage."

Some years later, she telephoned me. "I have good news for you," she said. She sounded very much alive and happy.

I said, "What is it?"

She said, "I'm calling to ask you to conduct a wedding for me."

"I can't imagine anything happier. You just name the time and place. I'll be there."

The "Model" Wedding

Her beauty was magical and magnetic. It was impossible not to look at her. And her beauty was not merely physical. It was almost unearthly, that of a pure spirit.

"I was born in Baltimore," she said. "My family were Episcopalian. In my adolescence I felt the need for religion and was not satisfied until I had made the rounds of the most representative and best-known churches. I was trying to find an answer. I wanted a faith. I felt that most of the religious services were too formal and dreary and hypocritical. The service in the temple was beautiful. I was most impressed by the rabbi—he is famous. You probably know his name."

"I do know him. But how long have you been in New York, and what do you do—what is your work?"

"I haven't been here long. I'm a model. But I've come to you because I expect to be married. The young man is Jewish. I've been to a few of your meetings, and I understand that you are nonsectarian. We have friends of many backgrounds. Do you marry people in our situation? Would you marry us?"

When I met the young man, I had the impression of the fast sporting type, the playboy. He was wealthy and handsome, graduate of an Ivy League college, a member of the right clubs. It was hard to see how he could appreciate and care for someone as sensitive and sincere as this breathtakingly beautiful human being. Admittedly, I identified with her, and would have done so no matter who the lucky man might have been.

On a clear and sunny late afternoon in spring, I went to a private house in the East Sixties. It was located on one of those blocks which have been kept unspoiled and beautiful. Most of the houses were built long ago, with beautiful designs and layouts for wealthy families who could afford rich surroundings, servants, and gracious living. When I entered the house I walked right into the bright lights of what seemed a stage setting for a Broadway musical. Against the light green walls and high up toward the ceiling young men in tails, striped trousers, and cravats were perched on ladders while others in tails held cameras and were taking pictures from this angle and that. A half-dozen young women from the Conover Modeling Agency, each in a beautiful gown, unique in style and color, smiled, turned, posed, displaying their charms and talents. This colorful scene of young men and women, all dressed as if about to launch themselves onto a stage, gave the impression of beauty, talent, grace, competence—but it also seemed to lack any deep personal relations of caring. They were a playboy crowd before the days of *Playboy* magazine and the Playboy Clubs. Doubtless some personal caring was there, but I felt one would have to be very strong and sure of oneself in such a crowd. I wondered whether the bride was being "had."

When all the pictures had been taken, we moved into the garden for the wedding ceremony. I remember the El nearby overhead. A train roared by during the ceremony. After the statement of commitment, everyone kissed. There were champagne and toasts, jokes and laughter.

After I left the wedding party, I walked westward across the park, carrying with me the afterglow of affection and feeling which the bride had expressed when she thanked me. I remember thinking that, beautiful and festive as the wedding party had been, something was missing. I could not get any human feel out of it. It seemed as if I was abandoning the one person who was most alone, most unsophisticated, most simple and honest and human. What was she being exposed to? Would she have a marriage and a home and a life?

For two or three years I heard nothing. Then one day the phone rang. It was the voice of a woman, weak as if she were very sick or at the bottom of a deep well. "Is this Mr. Black?"

"Yes," I said.

"You don't remember me, but you married me."

"What's your name?" I asked. She gave me her name. I said, "Yes, I do remember you. I remember the models and the beautiful garden. How are you?"

"Oh," she said, "my life has been nothing but suffering and tragedy. I felt I had to talk to you, to hear your voice."

"Tell me what's happened," I said. "Where are you?"

"No," she said. "You wouldn't want to look at me. I'm not the same as the person you married."

I said, "I'd like to see you. I'll come to you wherever you are. Just tell me, please."

"It's been horrible, but nothing can be done about it. But I do thank you for talking to me. It's good to hear your voice again. Goodbye." She must have hung up the phone.

I have not heard from her since. My attempts to find her have come to naught. That phone call haunts me. What could have happened to her? Was it the marriage? Was it something else? I have thought of it often. She was so beautiful, in every way.

When Parents Love

Before the wedding guests arrived, the mother of the bride, a former student of mine, asked me to join her in the library of their apartment. I remembered her as a beautiful teenager, active in student extracurricular activities, a leader warmly human with fellow students and teachers, always enthusiastic and of joyous temperament, a strong influence for unity and morale in the school. Now, happily married to a distinguished physician, she was a loving mother and in her home always offered generous hospitality to a large number of family, friends, and members of the medical profession. She was known and admired for her volunteer services to the hospital community.

She spoke warmly of her years at school and of her marriage and the many years of unbelievable happiness. Above all, she spoke of what her daughter meant to her and how fervently she wished for her happiness in marriage. Although she seemed to me even more beautiful than she had ever been in her teen years, it was evident that she was not well. There was a certain sadness mixed with her joy.

She left me to join her husband in receiving the many guests. I waited alone while the guests arrived. Then, when all were ready, the bride and groom and I walked into the room and faced the assembled families and relatives, elderly friends, and a large community of former schoolmates and college friends. In the moment of silence before I spoke, I was struck by the beauty of the light. It was not merely the sunlight coming through the windows. It seemed to stem from the mood of all those present, especially the parents and grandparents in the two families. It was reflected in the faces and the eyes of the affectionate young friends. It was a moment of almost unearthly communion.

I spoke briefly; the newlyweds exchanged rings and kissed each other. The mother was the first to put her arms around the bride and then around her new son. Embraces, kisses, handshakes, and congratulations. Then there rose a single clear, beautiful song. A girl with a guitar, as if moved by some hidden signal, filled the room with a simple ballad, a haunting expression of love.

A few months later, I was called to officiate at the funeral services for the mother. Not until then did I learn that she had known before the wedding that she had only a short time to live.

MEMORIAL
SERVICES

Notes on Facing Death

Birth and death are part of the mystery of life, part of the human condition. The important thing is not to fear death, but to fear not living. The real tragedy would be to know in the last days and the final hours that we had missed the most important thing in life, that we had wasted the years and had never used our gifts. For to live means to know the beauties of nature and of man's creations, the realities and processes of the natural world, the creations of the arts, and the joys of friendship, of loving and being loved. And to live means to become and feel part of the great human community. Being human should mean that we strive to live for the values which fulfill the human part and give life meaning.

It was said long ago that if we can overcome the fear of death, we can overcome the fear of life. If we do this, we can move through the years trustingly, filling each day with work and love, sharing the burdens and the joys of life with others. Then we can participate in the struggles of human beings to bring about a healthier and happier life for others and for ourselves. We can help to build a more decent, just, and peaceful world.

LOSING THE ONE WE LOVE

Every life is precious, every life in the world. But for each of us there are a few who have come very close and have shared our life. Their lives are especially precious.

We know that someday we will lose those we love. And the more

178

we love, the deeper our love, and the more intimately we share life, the more we suffer at death. Yet we would not be such cowards as to refuse to love for fear of being hurt someday. We love passionately, trustingly, generously, and courageously with all our being. Without love, life has no taste or fulfillment or meaning.

We grope for consolation. How shall we make peace and accept the loss of those we love? We have to find the strength and faith we need to go on—not merely to exist, but to live. When the one we love has lived a long life and a good life, has used life well and has known enjoyment and achievement and many fulfillments, then it is a little easier to face the reality that a life is ended. When one who was so alive and active, and now lies helpless and suffering, when one who was so alert and able to relate to the world, is no longer able to grasp the life around him, when he is no longer in command of his life, death can be a release and a blessing. These are times when we have to make peace with death.

There is consolation in the thought expressed by Socrates—that neither in life nor after death can any evil befall a good person. The one we love is beyond all passion and pain.

THREE WISHES AT DEATH

When we think about our own death, we might think of three wishes. And we may assume that the one we have loved might have had these same wishes too.

First, we would wish that those we love, those close in family and friendship, the neighbor and fellow worker, should understand what we lived for, our values and intentions, what we meant by our life at our best, seeing our faults and mistakes with understanding and generosity. We would want no eulogy or apology either.

Second, we would wish that our life had made a difference. We recognize how little one individual and one lifetime can mean in the totality of the generations. But we wish that because of us the world might be a bit different and a better place for man—with some lessening of fear and hate, some increment of good in man's struggle for a better life, something enduring beyond the finality of personal death.

Third, we would wish that those we love, whose lives are close, should not be confused or lost or depressed, unable to face the years ahead. Rather would we wish them the courage and faith to face the future with a clear sense of direction and concern for each other. For our life is tested in death by the way we prepared our loved ones to live without us, liberated from dependence upon us, free and strong to make a life when we are no longer there beside them.

IMMORTALITY

Why do human beings accept the belief in a life after death? Why do some believe that there is no death, others that we are resurrected, others that we are reincarnated in other forms, and still others that we live a life eternal in some other realm of existence?

Is it because men have such a fear of death, of the unknown, of darkness, of the strange? Is it because we hold life so precious, and our separation from the living becomes too painful to bear or imagine?

Is the idea of immortality a teaching to make death palatable? Is it to comfort human beings and deny the fact of nonbeing? Is it an illusion fostered to persuade the neglected and deprived, the exploited and oppressed of the earth, that everything will be made right in another life in another world? Is it the false promise to ease the pain of parting by promising that we will meet our loved ones again in another realm of being? Or is it a way of feeding and satisfying the egocentricity of the individual who believes he is so important that the universe owes him a foreverness—an infinite existence or an infinite series of existences?

Why not say: "I am grateful for my life. It is enough for me to have lived one life. Every life is meaningful in the linkage of life with life. I am one in the community that acknowledges the interdependence of all people and all the generations that have gone before and those that will come after." We are part of a cosmic process, some larger evolving reality of which we know not the beginning or the essence or the end. Every life is part of the whole. Everyone has a part to play. Every birth and growth and fulfillment and death means the enrichment of life, the dynamic interplay of unique individuals with unique combinations of qualities, and from that interplay growth and change and progress are possible.

Men die, but mankind lives on. Our immortality lies not in some myth of a nonphysical entity existing after the death of the physical body. It is a way of being which lives on in the lives of others. And if we touch the life of others creatively and lovingly, we have a life. This is the world of human beings, and it is through our relationship to others, and through the values we foster that we advance the unique potentialities of the human world for a better existence, a higher form of civilization, and, beyond that, the furtherance of the evolution of the human potentiality.

THE GREATEST GIFT OF ALL

We must ask in all honesty, "How does a man live after he dies?" The many different religions represented among us have offered answers to this question. But apart from all the differences of belief, there is one reality which we all. share, and on this we can all agree.

Sometimes the one we love brings us a gift bought with money, and we are grateful. Sometimes he brings us a gift which he created, the product of his own thought and: effort, something he-made with his own hands. This we. prize even more. But sometimes he comes close and lives with us and shares our joys and sorrows as if- they were his own. And. the more he is a distinct, person, the more he evokes our strength and the powers slumbering within us—the more we know that he is giving us the greatest gift of all : himself.

If he lives with us in a family or works with us day by day through the years, something happens to us which would not have happened if he had not lived and if we had never known him. For. his unique and distinctive personality lives in the way he touches our life. Because of his intelligence and power to think, we, in our own way,, are more alert and more able to deal with our, problems. If he works productively, we understand better what it means to be productive. If he has standards and values, we are clearer in our own standards and values. His integrity evokes integrity, in us. Because of his sense of humor, his joy of life, his laughter, we are better able to see things in perspective and to laugh and enjoy life. And if he is kind and compassionate, generous and loving, passionate for. justice, then we are more aware of these qualities and values in life. He will have helped us grow. He will not make us an imitation of himself. But he evokes our strengths, our talents, and' helps us grow. He helps us "get born."

And the wonderful fact is that when he dies, we don't lose what he gave us,, what he brought forth in us. He gave us ourselves. This is the way a person lives after he dies. It's real, not ghostly or mystical or sentimental. It is a truth which we can. all accept, no matter what theories we may have about an- afterlife in, another realm of existence. This, we say, is, true: we are better people because he lived. The. world is a better place because he lived; He gave us a great gift, his life, his influence, and his presence. We will treasure his image in our conscience and our consciousness. In darkness we will always see more' clearly because he lived. In difficulty and danger we will always know the courage he brought forth. And when we remember him, it will be as if he were present, and we will think more clearly and show more integrity and know more of what it means to love.

The Human Heart

The following passage is adapted from one of the
statements of John Love joy Elliott. The universal
response of people of a great variety of backgrounds
and conditions is evidence of the deep spiritual hunger in
people and the capacity of human beings to respond
without dependence upon the traditional creedal and
sectarian supernaturalism.

The love of the human heart is the most real and
    the most
Beautiful of all the realities we know.
It is the richest gift of our manhood and womanhood.
It is the love that joins us together as lovers, as hus-
    band and wife,
As father and mother, as parent and child,
And as friends and neighbors.
Whatever the length of time may be, to have known
    something of this
Is to have experienced the supreme privilege of
    being human.
The anguish of parting cannot destroy this most real
    of all realities.
The love has been,
The affection has existed,

The ties have been woven.
Life has been shared, the joys and the sorrows.
This has been as real and strong as anything in life.
The love that once was born can never die
For it has become part of us, of our life,
Woven into the very texture of our being.
Each of us would wish to leave some part of
    ourselves,
Yes, every one of us, some memory, some influence
    for good,
So here and now we bear witness to the one we
    knew in life,
Who now in death bequeaths a subtle part, precious
    and beloved,
Which will be with us in truth and beauty,
In dignity and courage and love
To the end of our days.

The Twenty-Third Psalm

One of the Psalms most widely known and loved in the Western world is the Twenty-third Psalm. It expresses something which touches our deepest needs at a time like this. It does so not because it is a revelation or makes a promise. It is poetry out of deep human experience, and this is why it conveys something precious beyond all creeds and rituals.

We do not know who created it. Was it a poet or a singer of songs? A king or a shepherd, a vagabond, a warrior? Some say it was a man named David, or a man who followed in the tradition of David. Some say the Psalm is of Persian origin, or out of the prophetic traditions of Israel. But scholars are not precise; the evidence is lost in the mists of history. Was the writer a man or a woman? What color of skin—black or white or brown? We do not know.

We do not know the language in which the Psalm originated. Whoever had the experience that moved him to the words and images that flowed out, possibly as he plucked the strings of a musical instrument—the language of that person was not modern English or French or German or Italian. Nor was it ancient Greek or Latin or Hebrew. It may have been an older language or dialect, older than all of them. Doubtless the Psalm was not written down at first. It was spoken and sung and passed from person to person and from generation to generation before it was written down. Now it exists in almost every language, in many countries.

Perhaps the question is not who created the Psalm or in what language. More important, why has it survived? I think we know why. It has lived because it meets a deep need, a deep spiritual need in human beings everywhere, a universal need in all places and for all ages. Where people are confused and lost and need to find their way. Where human beings lack confidence in themselves and need a sense of their own value and worth and the feeling that they can cope with their problems in the future. Where people suffer pain—their own and the pain of others—and long for life free from suffering. Where those who feel the senseless waste of life, long for something better beyond.

The thing to remember is that someone, thousands of years ago, had something within him, a deep spiritual security. He felt he could overcome confusions and feelings of weakness and of being lost. He felt strength, hope, and faith. He said with a full heart that he could walk beside the quiet "still waters." He could "lie down in green pastures" and feel that it restored and refreshed his soul. That he could find the paths of righteousness. That he could "walk through the valley of the shadow of death," and "fear no evil." That even in the presence of his enemies he felt that a table was prepared for him with food and drink. That his cup of wine "runneth over" and that his head was anointed with oil. Beyond all this, he felt that goodness and mercy would be with him all the days of his life. In its essence the psalm says, "I will find my way. I will overcome the difficulties of life. I am at home in the world of nature and the human world." More deeply than any words or symbols, this poem evokes a feeling of spiritual security. It is deeper than all creeds. It is saying that man can walk the earth in justice and love, with a faith in life.

As a closing word at a funeral or memorial service, or when people are very shaken by some catastrophe, I have found it fitting and helpful to speak this way about the Twenty-third Psalm. I have suggested that if the one who had died could speak, he or she would wish just one thing for us, the living, for every one of us who is left behind: that we should not grieve or be downcast. That we should not feel insecure or lost. We should be confident that we can find our way, and that whatever the days ahead may hold of difficulty or danger, we should know serenity, a feeling of at-homeness in the world, at-homeness with nature and with people. That, without a guarantee of a victory for everything that we hold sacred, we should still be able to enjoy the beauty and the goodness of life, by what we ourselves make of it.

Cremations

Although we all know that death is a fact of life, we still tend to avoid thinking about it. The death of someone close to us is almost always a shock. Even when there has been a long and serious illness, we are likely to be unprepared. In a state of emotional distress and anguish, and under the pressure of distraught relatives, we begin to be aware of the disruption of a life pattern and an unknown road into the future.

Prepared or not, immediate decisions have to be made. We find ourselves walking among the caskets at the funeral chapel. We select one and then sign papers for burial or cremation and other arrangements. Every day human beings are caught in such situations without information or guidance or any preparation for facing the basic fact of death.

The attitude toward death is not merely a theoretical issue. In the decisions human beings have to make about death, our philosophy of life is of crucial and practical importance. Even when people have a fairly well-worked-out approach to death, they are still at the mercy of grief, love and anger, guilt and sensitivity to public opinion. The decisions are related to the price of the casket, a grave, the choice of burial or cremation. How much are the wishes of the deceased to be respected? He may have wished that his body be given for medical research or transplant purposes. Religious traditionalists who believe in the immortality of the soul and the resurrection of the body, or relatives who believe there is no other decent way to respect the dead, may resist and reject any decision except burial. These attitudes affect decisions concerning funerals and memorials.

Religious traditionalists who believe in the immortality of the soul and the resurrection of the body still hold to the practice of burial in a grave. Many of the unchurched and nonreligious also tend to conform to traditional Western custom. Those who hold to a humanistic philosophy and faith are less tied to traditional procedures for disposing of the dead or a particular burial. Humanists are generally more open to the choice of cremation or the donation of the body for medical science.

In our Western culture and in the Judeo-Christian tradition we have accepted burial as a common custom. People quote from scripture: "All flesh is grass." If there is no burial plot in the family, the nearest of kin go forth to find and purchase a plot. In the great city cemeteries they find acres of graves crowded together, traditional symbols carved on gravestones, and, usually, a ghoulish atmosphere in bad taste, all of which makes it almost a sacrilege to leave there the body of one *they love.* It is even worse when the graves are so close and the earth so covered with industrial soot and city dust that no green grass is possible. Burials and cemeteries have become part of an outworn social custom, for visiting the gravesite is no longer common as a method of paying respect and tribute or of keeping alive the memory of a loved one. Modern families are dispersed all over the country and often live far apart. Whatevet values burial and cemeteries may have served in the past, today this is not the way to honor the dead. This is not the way to keep a memory and a love alive. Cemeteries are the waste lands. They are deserted by the living, and the dead are not there, either. They are symbols, not of remembering but of how quickly we forget the dead. Or they indicate that we know our deepest memory and love and gratitude were never really tied to the physical body. (If only the land were used for bird sanctuaries or recreation areas for young children, or set aside for beautiful garden homes for those who have never had any decent safe or beautiful shelter!)

We tend to accept without question the traditional and conventional customs of our Western world. But when we study history and the religious practices of other nations and cultures we realize that physical burial and graves and cemeteries are not the only way. A substantial part of the human race accepts and practices cremation.

When cremation is suggested, many religious groups naturally oppose it on theological grounds: how can people expect a resurrection of the body, if the body is burned? But the question which is never voiced is: what is realistic about the assumption that the body in the grave is preserved against the corruption and decomposition of the flesh?

Admittedly, some people are repelled by the idea of cremation, of flames touching the body of someone they love. Years ago, a friend of mine who turned away from the idea of burials and cemeteries, asked the director of a crematory, "Does it burn like a bonfire?" His answer was, "Have you ever looked into the sun? You know how bright and clear it is? That's what surrounds the body and consumes it. It's 'light like the sun.' " When she heard this she said, "My father's memorial does not lie in a mound of earth and stone. For me he will never die. He will be cremated, and I will give scholarships in his memory. To those unknown students who will benefit and grow, he will be bringing 'light like the sun' for generations."

At the Cemetery

The final physical parting is the hardest thing to face. There our most personal and warm feelings are tested and tried. For some this is difficult at the crematory. For others it is unbelievably difficult at the grave. Traditional ritual, whether it be the Kaddish of Orthodox Judaism or the prayers of the high Church, is affirmative with praise of life and thanks and praise to God. This meets a need. It is positive in the midst of feelings of loss and grief and separation. It channels our deepest feelings, helps us control our emotions. It assures that each one can turn to an outside reality which always was and always will be, an eternal and infinite absolute power.

We also praise life and the wonders of nature. The heart that started beating before birth and has beaten night and day for so many years, which has sustained life and intelligence and the will to live and to create and love—that heart is now still. There is no pain or suffering. Whatever the struggle for life, now it is ended. We have to make peace with this as we turn again to face life.

Two thoughts as we stand here at the grave: we are creatures of earth, made of the elements of earth. But we are much more than this, more than the chemicals, more than our parts. We give back to earth that which is of earthly origin. But we keep some precious part—the influence of the personality and the memory of the strength and character, of a mind and a sense of beauty, of the quality of relationships and the values which meant everything.

The other thought: a person does not occupy much space when he walks about on this earth. His height and weight and reach are limited, very limited. In the grave, too, he occupies very little space. But while he lives he occupies much more space than he fills physically. And in death he fills far more space than the grave itself. For he has moved about and reached out, seen and heard and acted and felt and touched other lives. So when we give back the physical part to the earth, we take away from this place far more than we leave behind.

The First Funeral

As part of my induction into the work of the Ethical Movement, I had been asked on a number of occasions to be present when older Leaders of the Ethical Society conducted funeral services. I had accompanied the bereaved family to the ceremony and had spoken at the grave.

Now the month was June; it was about 1930; I was the only one available when the call came to discuss a funeral service. A husband and father had died. He was Jewish in ancestry, his wife an Episcopalian. They had had a happy marriage for more than twenty-two years, with two wonderful children. He had left instructions that at his death he wished an "Ethical Service." I went to their home on Claremont Avenue on the hill near City College. When I rang the front doorbell, the seventeen-year-old daughter ushered me into the living room, where her father was laid out in a casket. We had hardly begun to talk when she said, "I want to tell you that I hope to meet my father again just as he is, just as I knew and loved him."

I was taken aback. I said, "I would like to help you and the family, but I'm not able to promise you what you want. I'm not even sure that you have thought through what you mean. If you were to meet your father again, I am sure he would want to meet you as a young man, the way he was at his best, not as an old man and not ravaged by illness as he was at the end. And I'm not at all sure that he would want a funeral service which would promise this. Although he was not a member of the Ethical Culture Society, I know he attended meetings and helped with the work. He was a Humanist, or he would not have left instructions to call us at his death. You and the family will have to decide whether you want one of us for an Ethical Service. If you believe in an afterlife and salvation in another world, perhaps you should have a priest of the Episcopal Church. He can honestly and with full heart speak the kind of promise you wish. I will walk around in the neighborhood for half an hour while you talk it over with the family. I'll come back, and you can tell me what you want."

With that, I left. After about half an hour I came back. The family decided to have an Ethical Service: "That was what Papa wanted."

After a long discussion with the members of the family, the wife and son and daughter and the brother of the man who had died, I left. Now I had to work out a service which would help his family face the death of one they loved and find consolation for their years ahead. There was no set service in the Ethical Movement. Each of the Leaders of the movement had to work out his own interpretations of Humanism and ethical concern for particular situations. It was difficult, more difficult than the carrying out of a given, set, traditional ritual. But, from the positive viewpoint, it was a challenge.

The two families, Jewish and Christian, had never been sympathetic
to the intermarriage and had never accepted it. This was confirmed by what I found when I arrived on Sunday afternoon for the service. The Jewish and Christian relatives were seated on opposite sides of

the center aisle. I began the service with some discussion of the man whose life was our common bond and whose life had brought us together. I spoke of the gift of life and the fact of death—that we should not fear death but should fear not using life well. I spoke of love and how we should have the courage to face the loss of those we love. Then I came to the part that I thought might be especially helpful.

I said: "Through the centuries, and through thousands of years, the Jews have said, 'Hear, O Israel, the Lord thy God, the Lord is One!'—meaning that we are all of one life, of one origin and one destiny. We share life together, no matter what there is of good or evil. There is enough suffering in the world. We owe it to one another to make life sweet, not bitter." This was my attempt to bridge the gap, to cross the aisle, to see if I could help to bring about some sense of tolerance and unity through the life and now the death of this man.

Then I said: "And the Christians through the centuries have said, 'I am the Resurrection and the Life!'—meaning, there is something in a man which never dies. In some sense the individual lives on. No matter what our differences are concerning theories of immortality, we know a man lives in his children, in his work, in his influence."

I thought that by my reference to the traditional phrasing of the prayer of Judaism and to the traditional phrase from the Christian creed, I could further understanding in the spirit of a truly loving family.

I had not realized how much each one hears the language that is familiar to him. An old Jew came up to me at the end of the service. He put his hand to his ear and said, "Vat synagogue?" I realized that he had heard the familiar "Sh'ma Isroel," the basic universal prayer of Judaism. I doubt that he heard anything else. The language made it kosher. He assumed that only a rabbi could have made such a reference. It is possible that some of the Christians heard only the familiar phrase, "I am the Resurrection and the Life," and had the same reaction. After the service a number of people from both sides of the aisle were friendly to me, as if they had found the service moving and helpful, and unique in that it was "beyond sectarianism."

Death as Tragedy

We have all experienced the sense of tragedy and sorrow when someone we know has taken his life. The sense of tragedy and grief is even greater when it is a young person. What possible consolation or comfort can there be when it is someone very close, a son or a daughter, a husband or a wife, or a dear friend? What could take away a person's will to live? What could make life unbearable? We cannot help feeling and thinking that the individual was beset by extreme frustration and pain. Do we not share some responsibility for this death? Yet I remember a few instances which still puzzle me.

A naval officer stationed at a base in Florida during World War II shot himself. He was a member of a distinguished family which had made many contributions to the cultural life of our country, a family of great wealth. His sister called me to ask if I would conduct a memorial service. The widow, when she arrived from the South, showed little grief. One could admire her for her control, but I found it very difficult to get any sense of love or a loving relationship.

I remember another occasion when a father welcomed me in his home. His love for his daughter was very great, and he was truly in agony over her death—and especially because she had taken her life. When he walked me into the room in which she had killed herself, he said, "We found an open book lying next to her on the bed. It was the Bible. It was opened to the Book of Job. If only she had turned the next page, and read what it says, she would never have killed herself!" What could one say to such a diagnosis and prescription?

I was greatly helped years ago by a funeral conducted by Dr. Donald Harrington of the Community Church. A beloved only daughter, beautiful and gifted, had taken her life. Her parents were professors at a great university, both having done distinguished work in their respective fields. The words that follow are my own effort to recall the imagery of that service.

"At times the reality we have to live with becomes difficult, very difficult. It is as if all we care about were endangered or devalued or destroyed. It may even seem to us that we can no longer cope with life, that we ourselves have lost the values of life, and even the value of ourselves. When we go through such a dark period of extreme frustration and pain, as we all do, we may find it hard to move in our accustomed day-to-day relations.

"We withdraw. We turn away from reality, sometimes even imagining more difficulty than there really is. We turn from the world, from family and those we work with, from those who love us. We swing far out in some way or other—far out and away by ourselves. And as we do this, it is as if we were in orbit around the earth, off the earth in great circles, getting some relief from having to meet the day-to-day realities which we find so unpleasant, even unbearable. After swinging out and away, we may come back to earth again and find it possible to make a new adjustment, new relationships, and a fresh start. We may have strength for that. Most people do. Or we may come back and swing out again, and then again, each time soaring further out and away until one day we cannot get back. We cannot return. The laws of gravity and the forces that draw us back to life and to each other can no longer overcome the outward thrust.

"So it is now. We know it in the tragedy of this beloved child. Her life meant so much. She had so much of talent and beauty, life to enjoy and life to give! It must be remembered in all its beauty and the fulfillments that she had, even though it was a short life. We cannot measure the value of a life by its length, or by the way it ended. Her personality and the values she lived by showed in her character and her devotion—possibly her too great devotion—to dreams and ideals which are not easily brought into reality. In her best feelings and her sense of possibilities, she felt defeated. We should remember her very much alive. We should forgive ourselves as we forgive her. With this we should find peace and solace in work, and in a concern for a world where every life is precious and should be treasured by all, that none should lose the taste for life or the will to live."

I remember a woman who called me to speak at the death of her husband. In the course of a long conference, days before the appointed memorial service, she revealed that he had killed himself. He was a gifted man who had done very well in a highly competitive field of business. The widow said that their marriage had been a happy one and that he had supported her through the years in her advanced studies. She knew that he was ambitious and had driven himself and had many anxieties because of competition and the instabilities of the market. Her sorrow and her grief were quite evident.

An hour before the service began, members of his family and hers, along with co-workers and friends, gathered in my office. The families were friendly in their greeting of one another. Conversation was subdued. Each spoke lovingly of the man who had died. When they had left my office to attend the service, the brother of the deceased drew me aside and took me back into my office. He spoke with bitterness and anger. "I must tell you," he said, "my brother was discharged from his position two weeks ago. He didn't want to tell his wife, because it might upset her. He had helped her to arrive at her profession, and she was just beginning to function. But just at the moment when he was most down because he had no work, she told him that he could no longer live with her. She actually put him out of the apartment. He took a room in a hotel, and took his life. I think you ought to know this before you speak at the service."

A Humanist service at death in such circumstances is not easy. How can one adequately help people go on living, forgiving themselves? How can we comfort and give support to the living for a new life with a new sense of responsibility and compassion and love? There is no one way. Personal situations, family relations, friends in the community—these are all involved. I have known three young black men who have taken their lives. They were former students of mine. I have been called for memorial services for refugees from Europe: Jews whose families had been wiped out and who were able, somehow or other, to come to this country, yet found that the taste and the will to live had gone out of life. The wonder is that so many are able to overcome the rejection and the persecution and the tragedy. These pages record some of the ceremonies of Humanism at death under especially tragic circumstances. They indicate the strength that Humanism can bring to the facing of tragedy, and the powers of people to endure and to help themselves and one another.

Stranger in the City

Marian had come to the city from a small Midwestern town. Her parents had worried about her. Could she make her way on her own?

She knew no one and had no connections. Could she take care of herself? From their viewpoint, the big city was a sinful place steeped in sex, liquor, drugs, and crime. But Marian found a place to live and a job—a good one. Within a few months she joined the staff and was made a junior editor of one of the best magazines for young women. Not only was she successful and recognized for her competence, but she continued to make many new friends. For the most part they were young writers and artists, the correspondents and readers who came in to talk with her, but they included people of every background, as well as the more sophisticated and better-educated. Her letters to her parents were enthusiastic, interesting, and encouraging. Those who were close to her felt self-confident because of her encouragement. No one had any reason to think that she might have some serious personal problems or a deep unhappiness. So it was a tremendous shock when she was found dead. She had taken her own life. There was no explanation. Was it a case of love betrayed or love exploited or love rejected? Perhaps somewhere there is someone who knows. But for hundreds of friends and her parents, the only reality was the agonizing fact that she was gone.

The first I knew of this, beyond the newspaper account, was when two young women asked for an appointment. They told me they were co-workers of the young editor. They spoke of her many friends and admirers, of the encouragement she gave to all, of her gifts, of her lovely apartment. "We all thought she was happy. It's hard to believe that she took her life. Some of us went to the church funeral back at her home in Ohio. It was a simple Protestant service with family and neighbors and a few former schoolmates. She's buried in the church-yard. But it doesn't seem right to us not to have a service here. She wasn't religious in the old ways; she was very open in her approach to all kinds of issues and people—people of different religions and backgrounds and colors. Would you conduct a memorial service for her here? We think her parents could be persuaded to come, and we would arrange to take care of them."

The memorial service was held on an evening. About 150 people came, young writers, friends, artists, staff members, and some devoted readers. The only older people present were her mother and father. The seats were arranged in two large circles so that we all faced one another. One friend played a Bach prelude. I welcomed the parents and the young men and women and expressed our shared sense of the linkage of life with life. Marian, out of her love of life and her feeling for people, out of her beauty and talent and hard work, had created a wonderful community of friends. She had overcome the impersonality of the city and the alienation which so many feel, by helping to bring forth the best in others, strengthening their courage and their confidence in themselves.

Then I called on those present to share some of their experiences with us, to talk of the things she had said and done, what she had meant to them, something about her that would help us all know her better and remember her.

One by one, young men and women stood up and talked about her, informally, spontaneously, sincerely. Some were successful; some were struggling young writers. She had come to mean more and more in their lives and careers. They had profited from her taste, her high expectations of herself and others. Whether she accepted or rejected their work, they benefited from her criticism and her encouragement. She gave guidance and affection and generated self-confidence. The last person to speak was the woman who took care of her apartment and cleaned for her. She paid a tribute to Marian's way of showing respect for others, to her standards of living as reflected in her home and her generosity and concern for others. She ended with the simple statement, "I loved to work for her."

It seemed to me that, as the parents listened, their expressions changed. The sense of utter tragedy, the memory of the suicide that brought with it feelings of failure and guilt to the family, was tempered by a new realization. They knew now that Marian had lived a full creative life and had reached out into a community of wonderful young people of talent and character; they knew that their daughter's life had had a quality of which they could be proud and happy. This was Humanism at its best. A stranger in the city had made a community and a communion of friends.

Andrew Goodman

In the summer of 1964 many young college students volunteered to help with the voter-registration campaign in Mississippi. Early that summer, three of the civil rights workers disappeared—James Chaney, Mickey Schwerner, and Andrew Goodman. After six weeks of search, their bodies were found in a mud dam; they had been murdered. Mrs. Goodman, Andrew's mother, phoned to ask if the funeral service could be held at the Meeting House. She indicated that Andrew's philosophy of life was Humanistic and that the family felt it would be appropriate to have the service at the Ethical Culture Society.

On Sunday, August 9, the Meeting House was filled to overflowing. Thousands stood on the sidewalk and along Central Park West. The parents of James Chaney and Mickey Schwerner joined the parents of Andrew Goodman. They sat together directly behind the casket. There was a single rose on the casket. Flowers, including three sprays of gladiolas, had been removed or turned back by the police because of a warning that we had better watch out for bombs in the flower containers.

I presided and spoke before introducing four friends: Martin Popper, attorney and friend of the family; Ralph Engleman and Barbara Jones, friends of Andrew; and Rabbi Arthur Lelyveld of Cleveland, a close friend of the family.

After we had all spoken, I added some closing remarks. The main address I gave follows.

We are people of all faiths—Christian and Jew and other faiths—and people of all colors. We are all of one life, of a common origin, of a common destiny on this planet. Whatever there is of good and evil in life, we share it together. We owe it to one another to make life sweet, not bitter.

This is a funeral which is joined with two other funerals of two other young Americans. These three funerals are part of a number of funerals that were never held, for those who have died in the cause of freedom—racial equality, freedom and equality for all men, regardless of color and regardless of creed.

In one sense this service is very personal. No one can know the agony of parents who bring a son into the world, who rear him, who see him as a beautiful person—gifted, with great promise, with a warm heart—and then see him cut down. No one can know this agony except those who have experienced it.

We all join in trying in some way to share this grief because it is also our grief. The blow that was struck at the body of this young man was a blow struck at the body of all of us—at the heart of all of us.

The wounds cry out. We ask, "Where is the conscience of this nation? Where is the decency? Where is the kindness? Where is the courage? Where is the integrity of the American people?"

We meet with a sense of shame and horror that there should be such racial bigotry, hatred, cruelty, brutality, ruthless violence against unarmed young Americans. Not in some other country, but here, under the protection of the Constitution, the law, the courts, the federal system of our democracy. We are speaking of the tragedy of a young life cut down. We are not just speaking of death here; we are speaking of life.

Life is not measured just in years, in length of time; the life of a man is measured by his acts, his feelings, his thoughts, his consecration, the quality of his life; and this is a proud death. This is a very proud death. It is based on unwearied love of man for man. We all desperately need the message of his life, the contagion of his faith, and the courage that he had to go and do, in that situation of danger, the things that needed to be done because he believed in the rights of his fellow men as well as his own.

Everyone who has experienced the thought and the feeling expressed here must have a sense of responsibility. It is very easy to blame other people for the ills of the world. It is very easy to talk about the other man's conscience, about his lack of citizenship, or how people have been silent and indifferent and apathetic. It is easy to criticize others for the ills of the world and for the evil that made this death. But if we are honest, and if we really have got the inner message of those who have spoken here this morning with such sincerity and depth of feeling, then each of us walks out of here with a responsibility.

The young people who are working in the South to help people learn to read and write, to help people pass the test for voting, to help people have the courage to go and register, despite the danger—those young people know about the funeral service this morning. They know that we are gathered here in tribute to Andrew Goodman; they know about the funeral that was held in Meridian, where people who call themselves Christians threw refuse at those who came to express their love and respect for the dead—for young James Chaney, and for Mickey Schwerner and Andrew.

The young people today in Mississippi and Alabama and other places in the South know about the service to be held tonight; they know that they depend on us for their very lives. They went down there trusting in America's promises; they trusted in the conscience of the people; they weren't asking whether you were Jew, Catholic, or Protestant, Negro or white, Republican or Democrat, rich or poor; they were trusting the people of America to stand back of them as they went, unarmed, to fight for the values they think make the world worth living in and without which they don't want to live and without which men have no respect; so there's a responsibility on every one of us. You can't walk out on it.

There are men who think they can kill and hide it, that the truth will never come out. But we live in a time when the truth comes out and people face it. If it doesn't come out and it isn't faced, then their life and their sacrifice is in vain. The news services have responsibilities. The government has responsibilities. But these and other agencies will not do their job unless we, the people, demand it of them; and it means that we must educate ourselves out of our own prejudices, so that America may survive in freedom.

So the question is not whether Andrew Goodman is dead; the question is whether we are dead. Wherever Negro and white stand up together, there will be the spirit of these three young men and all those who work for the fulfillment of their dream of democracy for all men. Wherever Negro and white fight for one another's rights, as for their own; wherever they break bread together, heal one another, teach one another, open doors for one another, enjoy life as neighbors, love one another; wherever this thing happens between us, there his spirit will live; and it must happen for every one of us personally—somehow or other to break down the wall, to let the light in that will make this world a fair place to live in and mean that this sacrifice is not in vain.

As we go from this place, may we remember that we would like it said of us, as we say of this dear son and brother and dear, dear friend: he was loved in his life and he has left undying love behind him at his death. He has made a great gift of his own precious lifeblood to the cause of freedom. May his kindness, his integrity, his courage, and his love be a blessing in the life of every one of us to the end of our days.

> At the end of the service, those gathered in the Meeting House and thousands in the streets outside joined in singing "We Shall Overcome"

Charles Abrams

Charles Abrams, an able lawyer, was involved in housing through his profession. Early in his career he became an expert on the relationship of housing to

community problems. 1 knew him as one of the
leaders and officers of the City-Wide Citizens'
Committee on Harlem from 1941 to 1947; then as an
officer of the New York State Committee and as
Chairman of the National Committee on
Discrimination in Housing. Through his work in the
area of fair housing, he became Chairman of the New
York State Commission against Discrimination. Over
the years his brilliance and amazing energy and
persistent efforts in research, teaching, writing, and
community action led him to become consultant to a
number of nations in Europe, Africa, and the Middle
East, and a resource expert for the United Nations.
Often we traveled together on trains and planes to
participate in hearings, conferences, and delegations.

The memorial service brought together not only his
family and many friends, but also public officials of
federal, state, and city departments, housing and
planning agencies, colleagues in law; and university
faculty members. It is impossible to reproduce what 1
said on this occasion. Instead 1 have included a brief
statement of my feelings and of the spirit of unity
which we all felt, and which is still a force in the lives
of many of those who knew him in many parts of the
world.

TO CHARLES ABRAMS

He is dead.
How can it be?
He was so much alive,
So much in love with life.

If a man lives alone
Just to himself
He dies alone
And the loss is his.

If he loves and gives his love
And is loved and belongs to others
His death is their loss too.

And if a man lives for all men,
If he binds himself to the community of friends,
What then?
We may all cry out
What right had he to die
What right to leave us now
When our need is great?

Yes, he belonged to all of us and we to him.
We were bound deeply, mind to mind and heart to heart.

He sat in his room behind his desk among his books
But no walls shut him in.
His mind's eye saw the larger citv, the region growing-
The flow of human life cut through the nation and the world.
He saw beyond the hands of his clock
Beyond the hour they pointed to—
Beyond the time ticking away the life of his generation.

His vision was the future.
There was no limit to the reach of his heart.

Alice K. Pollitzer_"Nanny"

Alice K. Pollitzer died at the age of a hundred and two
years. She was a graduate of Barnard College and a
devoted member of the Ethical Movement. She was the
wife of Dr. Sigmund Pollitzer. Her interest in children
led her to become Secretary of the Vocational Advisory
Service for Youth, and later Secretary of the Walden
School. She worked also with the Child Study Association of the magazine **Story Parade**. She had
marched in parades for womens votes and for peace.
In 1946, at the age of seventy-five, she helped to
found the Encampment for Citizenship and became

Chairman of its Board of Directors, a position which
she held for almost twenty years. After her death, the
memorial service was held on December 7, 1972, in
the Meeting House of the Ethical Society. In the
presence of her daughters' families and her many
friends, the service began with a trio for flute, oboe,
and cello played by three great-grandchildren. It was
the way she would have wanted to have a service, in
celebration of what was for her and for thousands a
creative and loving life. Afterward I spoke.

John Lovejoy Elliott often spoke of the fact that we
all are fortunate to have in our minds the images of a few favorite
people who have influenced our lives profoundly. Today we are trying to express our respect and love for one such human being who has
entered the life of each of us and has brought the warmth of human
affection and faith to thousands.

Nanny was one of those rare spirits who could go through the
world without being corrupted or depressed by it. She seemed to
have the inner strength that enabled her to stand against all kinds of
destructiveness. She seemed to have the kind of inner light that
made it possible for her to see her way even in darkness and to give
light that illuminated the way for others.

When we think of her, we think of Alice through the Looking
Glass. She believed the world was beautiful and that people were
lovely and lovable. She moved in a world of love. The reason is

obvious: she looked in the mirror—through the looking glass—for love and gave so much that it kept reflecting back to her. It was no wonder that she thought the world was lovely in so many ways, even when it wasn't. Her life in loving relationships made her more beautiful—made her more beautiful for over a hundred years.

Because Nanny's special grace of mind and personality brought out so much of the best in others, she, in turn, then saw and believed in the goodness she evoked. Hers was a very special paradise, this reflection which she created out of her own light and love.

When she was ninety she said
Who ever thought I'd live this long.

When she was ninety-one she said
I've had so much fun out of life.

When she was ninety-two she said
Every day is an extra bonus.

When she was ninety-three she said
I have no dread of death,
I guess the reason is
I've had so much of life.

> And when she was one hundred and one she said
> You know something?
> Love can keep you alive,
> Love can keep you young,
> And it can go on forever.

Some of us knew her as a very independent human being, a person who never was hard in the sense of being intolerant, dogmatic, or dominating, but very clear when she thought out what she thought. Some of us liked to fight, to differ and argue with her, and tease her. At times she seemed like a child, with her clear blue eyes and the way she looked at the world, and walked in the world of people. She was innocent, but not as a child is innocent. She wasn't ignorant. She wasn't unaware of evil and corruption and weakness and the false values around. We knew that we mustn't let her fool us. In her innocence she was also extremely sophisticated and shrewd and wise. She knew our strengths and our weaknesses. In the beat of her heart was the drumbeat of the feet of the children and youth of the world. Wherever there was struggle for a better life, she identified with it.

> After Bach's "Jesu,)oy of Man's Desiring" was flayed by Augusta Scheiber, pianist and friend, loving tributes were made by Mrs. Pollitzer's sister, Lucile Kohn, and a close friend, Allard Lowenstein. 1 then ended the memorial service with a message for the

grandchildren and great-grandchildren, and there was
a closing foem and song by Pete Seeger, folk singer.

And now I wish to speak especially to you who are
her great-grandchildren. She loved you very much. You must have
known that from the way she looked at you. She was very proud of
you. And she would have been proud to have heard the music this
morning, and the way in which you tuned up so carefully. You may
have been a bit embarrassed about that; I hope you weren't. It proved
what you are: that you know something about music, that you have
high standards of music, that you couldn't possibly play what you
were playing unless you came to certain basic agreements about the
trio you were playing and the tuning of your instruments. We are
particularly grateful to you that you took your time until you were in
tune the way you wanted it.

That's the kind of woman Nanny was. She would take her time
and have things the way she wanted them before she decided to do
something. That's why whatever she did with her life came out so
beautifully. Whether you are making a car, flying to the moon, or
playing a trio, you'd better have things right before you start. And
that's what she was about in her life, and especially in her relationships. Nanny was proud of you. She was proud of her daughters, and
the men that her daughters married, and her grandchildren, and their
children—you, the great-grandchildren—really proud. If we had
asked her, "What have you done with your life? What have you
made? Did you build a building? Did you fly to the moon? What did

you do?" I am sure she would have said, "Look at my great-grandchildren. These are my best, and I am in them."

When we last visited her in the summertime, she was sitting in the sun, looking out over the treetops and the valleys, the great open places. Some of you were kneading bread out in the sun. Some of you were making music. And some of you were out on the tennis court or going swimming. You were all around her. She loved you. She felt alive. Even though she could not walk easily, or see very well, she knew you were there. She heard your voices. She also felt your love.

So I hope you will always feel proud of where you came from. When you are old you can say, "You know, my great-grandmother, she was a real person. And if I have anything good in me, maybe some of it came from her."

She did not believe that you live after you die. Some people believe in a kind of soul that can exist without a body—that you live in some other kind of world, heaven or hell. And some believe that you are born again and again, in what they call "reincarnation." But there is one way in which we can all be sure that she lives, and one way we can be absolutely sure that we live after death.

If somebody loves us very much and lives with us, near us, and worries about us and helps us, and shares experiences with us when we are sick and when we are well, that person becomes part of our life. If she thinks clearly, then we too know what it means to use our intelligence. The more she knows how to laugh, the more we know the meaning of humor and fun and the joy of life. The more she is unafraid, the more we know what it means to overcome our fear and what it means to be courageous.

What we are has been influenced by the way Nanny touched our lives. We are more alive in certain ways. And when she dies we do not lose what she gave us. It is in us. We are different because of her, and that will be part of us as long as we live.

In ancient times people believed that when their ancestors died, they became stars shining in the sky. When they looked up at the sky at night, they were reminded of those they loved and those who stood for truth and goodness and courage.

We know there are millions of stars in the sky. They shine forth night and day. We cannot see them because of the bright light of the sun. But as the earth turns and we see the dark sky, we see the stars.

Long ago the poet Henry Wadsworth Longfellow wrote:

> "When evening twilight fades away
> The stars invisible by day
> Shine forth against the darkness of the night. . . ."

*

> So too at the death of one we love
> In the darkness of our sorrow
> The light of her life shines forth
> Clear and bright, warm, radiant, and steadfast,
> Lighting our way,
> Lifting our spirit and our courage,

A memory, an influence, and a presence
To be treasured to the end of time.

Death of a Baby

Before the funeral services for a very young child, it was difficult to say anything to console the parents. It was as if the young mother could not bear to see anyone, as if she could not bear sympathy even from those she loved. Pain and despair were in her eyes.

I fumbled with obvious phrases. Finally I said, "I wish I were a priest and could promise you that you will meet your child again in another life."

She looked at me out of the depths of her agony, her eyes indignant. "If I had needed or wanted that, I wouldn't have called the Ethical Society. I wouldn't have called you!"

Together we walked into the large room where families and friends had gathered. Standing before the little white coffin, I tried to express some of the feelings we all shared for a life so young that it had scarcely begun, and for a mother whose warmth and love had nourished the young life to no avail. When I spoke of the mother, her capacity to give and to sacrifice, to bear pain and to love and to overcome death, I felt a deep humility and gratitude for her courage and her spiritual integrity at the moment of intense grief at the loss of a beloved child.

Concerning the Child and Death

It seems to me that we should all be concerned to help children develop an honest and wholesome attitude toward death. At a number of funerals and memorial services I have been especially interested in speaking with children before and during the services for a parent or grandparent. They have always been interested and appreciative. Unfortunately, they are usually unprepared. In modern life we tend to shield children from any knowledge of death. We are silent and avoid the question as if it were as taboo as sex was until recently.

Throughout history, children have been exposed to death as part of life. In rural societies they have seen animals die. They have experienced the death of a parent or grandparent in their homes. They have attended funerals. They have seen men dig the grave and have stood at the grave when a relative was buried.

Today, the urban and suburban child may be more "protected." Conditions have changed in urban and rural areas. Families are more dispersed. Old people, especially grandparents, are more likely to live away from the family or with one branch of the family. When they are ill, they go to hospitals. They usually die there. And the children are kept away from funerals. We tend to excuse the practice by saying, "They are too young," or, "It's more important that they be in school," or "The trip from college would take time from the study for exams."

On more than one occasion I have said, "It doesn't matter how important school may be or the distance and expense; it's not kindness to deprive the young of experiencing the fact of death and the meaning of the death of a grandparent." When they have made the effort, neither the parents nor the children have regretted it.

For most children and youth, the only death they know is that which they see on the television screen. Of this they see a great deal. It is violent and brutal death. They have no identification with it. It is unreal. The only reality occurs when they meet it head on—on the highways. Even then they are unprepared. For many it may still seem unreal, an accident, not part of the life of all of us.

I remember two couples that I married, both very happily; each had two or three children. In one case where the mother came down with cancer and was in the hospital, the father talked very frankly to the children about the mother's illness. He explained how serious it was. Each time he visited the hospital, he took them with him. The mother was remarkable, in that she knew the illness was probably terminal and she was well prepared to face her death without fear. We talked about this when I visited her. When the husband and children visited her, she talked about the possibilities very quiedy, and about what they would do when she was gone. When she died, I spoke at the funeral. Somehow, it seems to me, those children were prepared in a quiet and courageous way, geared to the reality of death, and better prepared for life.

In the other case, the father tried to shield the children; he told them almost nothing except that the mother was ill and would be away for a time. The children were torn with anxiety. Since they did not dare ask their father, they asked other people. A number of friends and relatives were quite upset, not knowing how to answer the children.

I remember an incident a few years ago, when the Society had very young children at Camp Felicia, up on the west side of the Hudson. It was a summer vacation camp and drew children mostly from the low-income groups on the West Side of New York City. One day the director of the camp received a message that the mother of one of the children had died. The family was Irish Catholic. The director called the child in and tried to explain about life and death, how every flower and every tree grows and matures, how the time comes when it is old and it dies. He used other examples from nature and the animal world. The child was inconsolable. Finally, one of the mother aides who was present at the camp came in and took the child in her arms and rocked him and said, "Your Mommy is with Jesus. She's in heaven watching over you and waiting for you. You will be with her again." The child was comforted and quieted. He was consoled according to his tradition.

We have an obligation to prepare children today to face the fact that we lose those we love and we must find ways of living on, treasuring their memory and their influence, striving to keep faith with what they stood for and lived for, and what they wished for us.

At noon in the middle of my Ethics session with the senior class of the high school, the phone rang. "This is Dr. Grossman, Mr. Black, I am a former student of yours. I am a resident at Memorial Hospital. Last night I admitted a very young child ill with leukemia. The child may not live out the year. When I asked the parents their religion, they said they were members of the Ethical Culture Society. If it were a Catholic family, a priest would be here to meet them at visiting hours. I thought I ought to tell you."

I thanked him and asked, "What time are the visiting hours'?" He answered, "At two p.m." "I'll be there," I said, "and thanks for calling me."

I was there to meet the parents and walk with them as they pushed the stroller with their little son back and forth among the other couples who faced the same tragedy. The doctor had told me, "There are a thousand laboratories working on the problem of cancer and leukemia, and other dread diseases. They may find the answer in time, but it isn't likely."

At the funeral service, family and friends were there to give support and sympathy. How could they make sense out of the death of one so young, so unfulfilled? How to alleviate the parents' agony, the mother and father who loved him so and worked so hard, both of them, to make a home and a future for their children?

In more than one situation, I have counseled parents not to permit their grief to upset their relationships and their love for the child left living.

Where parents, and grandparents too, are overcome with grief at the death of a child, it is important to remember and love the child that is left.

Forgive me for intruding
On your grief.
To try to comfort you
Would be presumptuous,
Yet, knowing your tragedy,
I would speak.
Love can heal,
Love can wipe out the memory of evil,
Love is stronger than death.
You have another child,
Do not crush her with your grief
Or overwhelm her
With your sorrow.
I too have lost a child,
An only one—
There was no other

Just as many people, especially parents and members of the medical professions, have hesitated to let children know when a parent, a grandparent, a favorite teacher or doctor is seriously ill or dying, so they have hesitated to inform children when they themselves are seriously or terminally ill.

Children who are dangerously ill or facing terminal illness tend to sense that they are in danger. The expressions on the faces of parents or the weeping of parents may alert them. The silence or evasion of their questions adds to their anxiety. Although no one has the right to generalize for all individuals and age levels, it seems to me that greater honesty may be helpful to children.

In recent years, increasing numbers of the medical and psychiatric profession have deemed it wise and right that children in such situations should be carefully prepared and honestly informed of the possibility of their own deaths. Much is being thought and written about this subject. The following passage is one which has meant a great deal to me:

"The truth can be told to children in graded doses, and the child seems to be happier if he knows where he stands. This is illustrated by the case of the five-year-old boy described in James Knight's paper on 'Philosophic Implications of Terminal Illness.' The boy suspected from the tragic expression on the faces of his parents that he was going to die. He asked one of the doctors if this was the case. His doctor told him honestly that he was very sick and that so far the treatment had not been very effective. He asked the boy gently if he was afraid, and the boy returned the question. They both decided that they were not. The following day, when the boy's parents visited him in the hospital, he told them that everything would be all right, no matter what happened, and that they should not worry. They asked, 'Why do you feel this way?' His simple and moving reply was, 'Because my doctors love me.'

"Usually the child has family and friends around him and does not suffer the isolation and aloneness that many adults experience.

Thus he belongs to the group, and the sense of solidarity and community of the group is never broken for him."1

Live a Little Longer

I will never forget Allan Edman, a youngster who had gone through the religious education program of the Ethical Society and had been a member of the teenage groups. In the self-governing structure of the youth groups, he was elected an officer. In school he was a good student, editor of the high-school paper, and involved in community services. He was good in athletics. Outside school he earned his own spending money by bringing eggs in from Long Island farms for a group of regular customers. He was bright, energetic, interested in music and photography, wonderful in his relations with his own peer group as well as with older people.

In his senior year in high school he became ill with cancer. The doctors said he would be dead within a year. They did everything they could to ease his discomfort and pain, but at that time there was reluctance to be honest with patients, both old and young, when they faced terminal illness.

---

1 From a paper by James A. Knight, M.D., on "Philosophical Implications of Terminal Illness," quoted in *Counselling the Dying* by Margaretta Bowers, Edgar N. Jackson, James A. Knight, and Lawrence LeShan (New York: Thomas Nelson & Sons, 1964).

During my visits at his bedside, Allan and I had many discussions about family, teenage behavior, friends, current events, and basic values. There came a day when I thought it might be helpful if Allan joined the Ethical Movement. It would give him a feeling of identity, a sense of commitment to something greater than himself. It might be a source of joy and satisfaction to his parents. It might be helpful for him to know that he had this kind of bond with others, and with a movement that would go on after his death. So I said, "Allan, I know that you have great respect for the philosophy of Humanism and work of the Ethical Culture Society, I wonder if you have ever thought about associating yourself as a member."

Allan looked up at me from his bed. His eyes were bright and filled with enthusiasm for life. He said, "Yes, I've thought about it a lot, especially lying here and reading and thinking all these weeks. I must tell you that if I were ever to join any movement, it would certainly be the Ethical Movement. But don't you think I'm too young? I'd like to see the world, move among different kinds of people. When I'm at college, and after college, then I could make a choice and I'd know what I was doing. Don't you think I ought to live a litde longer?"

What could I say? I replied, "You're right. If you had come to me and said, 'I'd like to join,' I would have answered, 'Live a little longer,' just as you have. But I thought since you've been ill for such a long time and unable to come to meetings, you might feel close and justified in joining us. But I respect your viewpoint. Some other time we'll talk about it."

Allan's condition worsened. Drugs made it impossible for him to maintain consciousness. At the funeral service, two of us spoke: Dr. Irwin Edman, his uncle, a professor of philosophy at Columbia University, and myself. Family, fellow students, teachers, club members, club leaders—many people who respected and loved Allan—were present. My remarks were as follows.

"Those of us who knew Allan know that in his short life he lived more than many people who have lived many decades. In a very short time he lived at least five lives. His photography, his music, his studies, his business, his friends—each area represents his tremendous vitality and unique personality. He would want no wailing or lamentation, but he would want us to find peace together as he has found peace. Peace that goes beyond the passions and the pains of life. Peace which is on him and on us.

"Allan had a rare feeling for older people. He was unusually intelligent and wise for his years and had deep religious feelings. He was the kind who asks questions, reaches out to grasp the world. He cared deeply not only about his own life and the members of his family, but also about the many friends he made among his peers and his teachers. Even during the months of suffering he found it possible to have a vivid interest in world affairs. He was particularly concerned about whether the world would go to war. As a thinking youth, he saw the tragedy ahead and longed and hoped for its avoidance.

"One great source of satisfaction to those who knew him was the fact that this shy, sensitive, modest boy could have such friendship and loyalty from others and could be chosen again and again for responsible office. People instinctively trusted him.

"There is an integrity about selfhood which, when it is that honest and clean and fine, nothing can injure. By his faith in the strength of selfhood, he brought out in the people around him such decency, such generosity, that he really strengthened our faith in what *might* be among people. I think he has given us a love and a faith in things that we can treasure to the end of our days. No matter what happens to us, our memory of Allan should shame us in any weakness and strengthen us in any crisis, for if there is one outstanding quality that showed especially in the last months, it is the courage with which he took what came to him. In the midst of his own suffering he made a special effort to conceal the pain that would give others pain. He was particularly considerate and particularly grateful, far beyond what most of us are capable of. If a person can live forever in any sense by his sheer strength and fineness, then Allan achieves what few of us will have achieved.

"His death is a tragedy. But I wish to say again that he lived joyously and fully, and that we should be happy with this, happy that we were part of his life and that he was part of ours."

I ended the funeral service with a quotation I had adapted from Shelley's *Prometheus Unbound:*

> To suffer woes which hope things infinite,
> To forgive wrongs darker than death or night,

To defy power that seems omnipotent,
To love and bear,
To hope till hope creates from its own wreck
The thing it contemplates,
Neither to change nor falter nor repent,
This is to be good, great and joyous,
Beautiful and free,
This alone is worthy of thee,
In this alone is victory.

In World War II many of the young men in our clubs and classes at the Ethical Society and the Ethical Culture Schools volunteered for or were drafted into the armed services. Many came into the Meeting House and asked if they could join the Ethical Society. They knew they were going to be asked what their religion was, so that their dogtaes mieht be properly marked "Catholic," "Protestant," "Hebrew," or "Other."

"I want to put down 'Ethical Culture' as my religion. I want to join the Ethical Society. As I look at life, that's where I stand." I gave them membership application forms. These were my former students. They knew they were going out to face possible death. Before the war I would have said, "Why don't you live a little longer?"

230 – MEMORIAL SERVICES

While We Are Young

While we are young
Let us care for love tenderly.
It is not enough to carry memories
Of sun and garlands,
The moon in the night sky.
It is not enough to carry memories
Of the passion
That shook the earth
And carried us into outer space.
Too soon the day will come
When we will see only the darkness
And the distant stars
And know our loneliness

Jane

Jane was a former student of mine. I conducted her
wedding service. This was a love marriage out of
the ordinary, and the couple's happiness knew no
hounds when Jane became pregnant. For Jane's
husband and the two families and a large number
of friends, her death in childbirth, when she was
twenty-six years old, was devastating. Yet the love

was strong and wide-spread. I spoke at the funeral
service as follows.

If ever there was a time when we needed to take
hold of ourselves, to have strength, to see life whole, it is now. We
cannot deny, or ignore, or hide from our tragic loss and the pain of it.
Nature is cruel. We pay a price for living. We must be strong
enough.

We have the strength to speak of Jane simply and calmly. We
gather in a kind of communion in and through our bond with her, in
the love as well as the pain which strikes deep into us at this
moment, in the fact that we feel closer to her now than ever before,
with perspective on her life—her words and acts, intimacies and
memories.

Some knew her as a child—responsive, inventive, gentle, attractive, cooperative in work and play.

Some knew her as a good friend, a good companion, good fun,
vivacious and at the same time gentle and sweet.

She was an affectionate sister, a devoted daughter. And in her
marriage she reached the climax of her happiness and was able to
express her vitality, her gaiety, her love of the out-of-doors, of the
wind and the ocean, the enjoyment of books, the theater, and, above
all, of love. Then into her life came the greatest promise of all, the
possibility of a child. And with this sense of fulfillment, a young life
ended.

Those who were closest to her, her dear friends and family, brought her happiness; they joyously gave her support, security, and affection. She brought forth from them the power to give—generosity, truth, and affection. She has blessed all of us by being what she was.

Were she to speak, she would say, "Weep not for me—but do remember me." Above all she would want us to be certain things to one another, to her husband, to her sister, to her parents. To that dear circle of friends.

We can take many lessons from her life—the sense of self, the feeling of human solidarity.

May it be said of us when our lives are ended: the memory of this dear child, beloved wife, and good friend shall be a blessing upon us as long as we live, and on the lives of our children and our children's children.

Harold Weston, Conservationist and Artist

There were three parts to the ceremony: the prepared tributes and interpretations of his life; spontaneous tributes from individuals in the spirit of a Friends Meeting; and my remarks, addressed to his fifteen grandchildren.

I welcome you here to this Meeting House of the Ethical Society. We are gathered to pay tribute to a most unusual man and a dear friend, one whom we admire and hold in affection and love, and to whom we are all grateful. I should tell you—if you do not know it—that S. Burns Weston, father of Harold, went to Antioch College. He was graduated about 1876, went on to Harvard Divinity School, and was ordained as a Unitarian Minister. In no time at all he underwent a heresy trial in the Unitarian Church, left it, and was much influenced by Felix Adler, who had, in 1876, given lectures in New York on the possibility of ethics as a religion, a Humanist approach to faith. S. Burns Weston gave a series of lectures in Philadelphia in 1885. From this began the Ethical Culture Society in Philadelphia. So the Weston family has roots back in the Free Religious Association and the Ethical Movement, the forerunners of this Meeting House and the Ethical Societies in the United States. Needless to say, we are close in spirit to Unitarianism and the Friends, sharing a liberal and rationalist approach to a philosophy of life.

So it is quite fitting that we have this service here for a family that has been very close to us for generations.

If I may tell an amusing story at a time like this—Harold Weston had a wonderful sense of humor. When he was quite ill, even after he had had polio, he made some daring international trips. In Persia, when he was dangerously ill, the physician who was trying to help him was apparently more concerned about how to bury him than how to heal him. Was he Hindu or Muslim or Christian or what? On the answer would depend the disposal of his body. According to the story, when he was asked what his faith was, at a moment of very high fever when he was barely able to speak, he said, "Ethical Culture." Perhaps this makes it even more appropriate to hold this memorial service here.

I would like to share a passage from John Lovejoy Elliott. He wrote: "The love of the human heart is the most real and the most beautiful of all the realities we know. It is the richest gift of our manhood and womanhood. It is the love that joins us together as lovers; as husband and wife, as father and mother, as parent and child, and as friends and neighbors. Whatever the length of time may be, to have known something of this together is to have experienced the supreme privilege of being human. The anguish of parting cannot destroy this most real of all realities—the love has been, the affection has existed, the ties have been woven, life has been shared, the joys and sorrows, and this has been as real and strong as anything in life. The love that was once born can never die, for it has become part of us, the very texture of our being. Each of us would like to leave some subtle part of ourselves."

Isn't it important that we should be able to say at the end of our lives, I have lived, I have created, I have loved, I leave some influence for good? Whatever the hardship and suffering, whatever the frustrations and my own inadequacies, there have been moments that have justified my life. I have been a man in the years I have had. I have been a woman in the time I have had. I have not been afraid to live, and I have not been afraid of death. I have not been afraid to love, even though I have lost those I love. I have known joy and sorrow. I have known what it means to be human. We would all like to be able to say this, and we would also like to believe that we have made some little difference, some positive contribution to the common life. I think this is true of Harold Weston. I do not think he feared death. He had a great lust for life. He wanted to create, and he did. He wanted to have impact on the life around him, the larger life, and he did. We are part of the evidence, and we are only a small part of the larger human world that he touched.

Because Harold Weston loved the Adirondacks, the mountains, the woods and streams, and because he fought to protect them, Morgan Smith will speak as President of the Adirondack Mountain Reserve. And because he loved beauty and gave support to those who work in the arts, Lloyd Goodrich, Vice-Chairman of the National Council of the Arts in Government, and William Smith, President of the United States Committee for the International Association of Art, will speak of Harold Weston's work and his creative contributions.

> After these presentations, a number of friends spoke
> spontaneously, each relating some recollection of
> Harold Weston as a person, a friend. Following these,
> I addressed the closing remarks to the fifteen grand-
> children ranging in age from five to twenty.

In bringing this memorial service to an end, I wish to say a personal word to you, the grandchildren of Harold Weston. I want to remind you that your grandfather was not always an old man. You knew him only at the end of his long life. I wish you could imagine him as he was at the beginning of his life, when he was young. He might have liked you to remember him as he looked and walked and did things when he was young like yourselves. Most of us who are here today, and have gray hair, knew him when we all were young and when he did many of the things that you do.

He loved the mountains and the woods. He climbed the mountains and he walked the trails and smelled the pines and spruce trees and felt the soft damp forest earth with his feet. He fished in the fast-running streams. He cut wood to build houses and to make warm fires. In winter he cut ice. He loved to look up at the sky, at the clouds over the mountains, the storms too—black thunderheads and flashing lightning—and he helped put out many forest fires. Your grandfather loved beauty. He loved all living things, colors, lights, forms, the wildlife great and small.

I think he just loved life. He wandered out on the land. If he ever was afraid, he overcame his fear. Then he fell in love with Faith, your grandmother. In his book, *The Free Wilderness,* there is a photograph of both of them cutting a tree down, pulling the saw back and forth—a big tree, seven feet around. It is important to remember your grandparents. They were young and had fun and loved beauty and lived with courage.

Your grandfather loved to paint. Whether he was a great painter or not is not so important. He loved to paint, and he loved painters and helped them to paint. He helped the artists of the world. He built a house up there in the Keene Valley when there were almost no other houses. He was strong and tough in the woods and stood up for what he believed.

Such a man can be a tough father at times. If a father is strong and tough, he may dominate and make his children weak. But he also can bring out their strength and make them strong. Boys and girls go through times in life when they do not always agree with their parents. We all have to become strong, to find out how to behave for ourselves and think for ourselves and learn how to live. Sometimes we have to differ with parents and fight with them. That's all right, if we grow through it and if we still love each other.

What shall we think and what shall we say when a person dies? There is one way we can all believe about the way we live after we die. Some people live more after they die than other people because they lived more while they lived and touched other lives.

Now, if a man loves you, cares about you, and lives with you— when you are sick and when you are well, when you are sad and when you are happy—if the man who loves you and touches your life has a good mind, you know how to think better. If he loves beauty, you will know what beauty means, more than you would if you had never known him. If he has a good sense of humor and can laugh, then you learn how to laugh better. If he knows how to love, you know what it means to love better.

It does not mean you become like him. But he helps you become more of you. The wonderful thing is that, when he dies, you do not lose what he gave you: he gave you yourself. What he gave you will be with you all the rest of your life.

As we leave this place, we will carry with us in our memory the image of this man—his smile, his walk, his voice, his laugh, his courage, and his faith and his great love of life and love of people. He gave his love for the generations that were going to come after him. May we treasure the wilderness as he did and may we protect the beauty of the world. And may we be true to his spirit and his memory.

While 1 was s-peaking I noticed that one of the very youngest of the grandchildren, a little towheaded boy sitting toward the front of the Meeting House, was nodding at my references to his grandfather and wiping his eyes. When 1 finished my remarks, he raised his hand. 1 asked, "Did you want to say something?"

"Yes."

"Will you come up here on the platform?"

He stood and walked forward. I placed him in front of the microphone so that he faced the more than two hundred people who were attending the service. Then in a small hut clear voice he said, "I have a story—we were up at the Upper Lake, and people, my grand-mother and my mother, were up there, and Grandpa

brought in a deer and he gave it sugar. And Grandma
and Mommie didn't exactly like it. But he sure had a
way with all the animals."

With that, he burst into tears.

1 thanked him for all of us.

Funeral at Arlington

Norman E. Himes was a distinguished scholar, teacher,
and devoted citizen. In the Second World War, as a
major in the office of the Surgeon-General of the Army,
his assignment was to write a medical history of the
war. When the war was over he was sent abroad, where
he died in Venice, Italy, in January 1949.

His body was brought back to the USA. He was to
be buried in Arlington Cemetery. In preparation for
the service in one of the chapels, 1 spoke to the officer
in charge. I said that Norman was unchurched and a
Humanist. It would not be appropriate or in keeping •
with his spirit to have a cross or any other religious
symbol at the service. The flag on the casket was ample
symbol.

The number of persons who attended the funeral
service was beyond expectation. Among them were
Army personnel and government officials, members of

the medical profession and the National Council of
Maternal Health, and the officers and workers for the
Planned Parenthood Federation of America. There
were also some members of foreign embassy staffs and
international commissions, members of the Washington
Ethical Society, and members of the family. I spoke as
follows.

Norman Himes is known to every one of us as a
man who gave his life for a better life for all of us, not with guns but
with learning and the uses of knowledge for a more ethical life in our
country and among the nations of the world. I am sure that everyone
here from the Army, from the fields of education and social services,
from the field of international relations, had respect for him as a man
of intense patriotic loyalty. He was a citizen with a passion for
democracy, a man devoted to a kind of scholarship that would help
people live in greater freedom and equality. He was a devoted and
loving husband. He was a faithful friend.

I speak of him as a classmate at Harvard University and as a close
friend and a fellow member of the Humanist movement. He was
deeply imbued with the best in Christian ethics. In his studies of
sociology at Harvard he began to see the importance of population
control as a national and a world problem. In his research studies of
the history of birth control, he uncovered the contraceptive methods
used by the advanced cultures of thousands of years ago, the ancient
Egyptians, Greeks, and Romans, and down into modern times. His

work led him into anthropology and medicine and also led him to understand the implications of birth control, the need for more honesty in attitudes toward sex, healthier and happier marriage relationships, and causal factors in mental and emotional health. In overcrowded nations and in overpopulated earth he saw causes of wars. He saw wise contraception policies as a necessity for peace.

Because of the soundness of his research and his ability to write, his books—*The Medical History of Contraception, Your Marriage,* and *Practical Methods of Contraception*—helped inform and liberate an entire generation in the United States and other countries. He became a member of the faculties of Clark University, Colgate University, the University of Colorado, and other schools. He was a teacher who influenced more than one generation of sociologists. He was consultant to the National Council on Maternal Health, a Director of the Population Association, and a member of the National Conference on Family Relations.

At the end of the war he was sent to Europe to direct education in the orientation of troops, and later he developed programs for the reeducation of the German people and worked at this task from 1946 to 1948. In the International Conference of Youth in Munich in 1947, he said to German youth, "Stop pitying yourselves. I find a great number of people saying that Germany cannot become a democratic and peaceful nation until everyone is well fed, well housed, well, clothed, and so on. In the final analysis, the vitality of the democratic form of life depends on the conviction of its inhabitants that individual liberty is worth even temporary economic adversity."

What he said to them then applied also to many Americans and to the people of nearly all countries.

The effort of his life has been to heal illnesses, to help family life and marriage become more fulfilling and responsible. He believed and taught that every child born in the world should be born wanted, provided for, cared for, and loved. Back of all that he did, he understood the lessons of the *Essay on Population* written by Malthus in 1791, lessons that had to do with human suffering from famine, plague, poverty, and war. That essay was as important for the future of mankind as any of the writing of Darwin or Marx or Freud. For Norman Himes that essay became a guideline to his career and his life. The children of the future, the marriages and families of the future, will reap the benefits of his work.

Norman lives in his books, and he lives in the lives of all of us who were his classmates and friends, and in the countless human beings who were his students and fellow workers in the struggle for a world which will respect human values. As a Humanist, he joined the Ethical Movement and was President of the Washington Ethical Society. The Ethical Society in the nation's capital owes its existence in large part to the vigor and devoted leadership he gave it in the war and postwar years. He held that man is saved by his own respect for the laws of nature and the uses of human intelligence and conscience to transform life and to fulfill human potentialities. He will live in the hearts of all of us who knew him: his beloved wife, his family, and his friends. May his concern and love for us be with us and help us live with courage and commitment to the human values which give life its deepest meaning.

From the chapel we walked behind the caisson
carrying the casket. At the grave the following words
were said.

As he was faithful in life, so we who were close to
him in life have gathered together at his death to express our appreciation of the kind of man he was and our gratitude that we have
been able to share life with him. The tremendous respect which we
feel and which this nation owes him is symbolized by the burial of
his physical part in this earth hallowed by those who have made
heroic sacrifice for the nation and have paid with their lives. Here we
pay homage to his spirit. May each springtime bring forth the
warmth of the sun, and raise up the grass and flowers from this earth
to make beautiful this hillside. So too may his spirit be regenerated
in each of us, in our life and work, in the years to come. We shall
treasure the values he lived for and the values he embodied in his
heart and spirit.

Carl Ramsey and the Star Orchid

After World War II, in the years of my weekly
broadcasts called "Ethical Issues in the News," one among the radio
fans wrote me at least once a month. The address on his letters was
Swampacres—Wild Life Refuge, Dorset, Vermont. I gathered that
he lived in a simple shack under somewhat primitive conditions on a

bit of dry land adjacent to the swamp. With him were his wife, Edith, and his daughter, Margaret (Peggy). Much of his time and energy was spent gardening and fishing. But his greatest joy was his life in the swamp. There he established relationships with birds and small animals. He fed them, named them, observed and wrote about them. As for plant life, he had one grand passion—prize orchids.

Although he was close to his wife and daughter and his immediate neighbors, he was a maverick in the midst of the larger conservative community. No doubt the people generally thought of him as a recluse and at the same time, because of his social outlook, as a social radical. He did his own thinking and he spoke out freely.

As our friendship grew, my file became full of his writings. A few fragments from his letters offer some indication of his love of nature, his feeling for beauty—and his struggle to live.

October 1944: "I'm afraid you were needlessly apprehensive regarding myself. I'm glad Edith told you of the hectic round of summer; there is simply no time for anything, once I get into the planting of the garden. I feel the importance of producing as much food as possible for ourselves and of course I sell the surplus to a few intimate friends and those who happen to hear of the garden and come in to pick it up. My fishing orgies are a form of escape though actually something more than that, for the communion of Nature goes with it and while I am glad to replenish the larder, it is a joyful procedure that is an essential phase of my well-being. No verbal description of our beautiful mountains can possibly convey their actual charm unless you have been among them as I have for over a score of years now. It has been a veritable university to me for there is always something new and delightful turning up in these various excursions. I'm afraid I am not a simon pure city dweller—there is something of the Indian in my blood and I hanker after the wild."

October 1944: "I could have hugged you for a number of things that you said in your various radio Ethical Issues talks—the one on the President and the one on Wallace in particular struck harmonic notes. I am a bit worried over the forthcoming election though maybe I shouldn't be for even the common man in spite of his abysmal unschooled approach to political and economic questions is essentially sound."

Jawuary 1954: "We are still without electricity though we have a little bathroom that functions at the throne via a pailful of water from our hand pump. Like Thoreau we have embraced the philosophy of not wanting anything we can't pay for or 'wanting little' as Thoreau put it. I needn't tell you that it is a cock-eyed world and I don't know where in hell we are going to land if the McCarthys, Dulles, Ike plutocracy have their way. The whole thing doesn't make any sense, and it seems more difficult all the time to tell people just that. I don't mean just the average Vermonter but I have college bred women tell me I ought to go to Russia.

"I keep plugging away at my major work with the orchids which seems far removed from any contact with humanity. Still, the gospel of the orchids as I see it has great significance if for instance the necessary funds could be gotten to develop the visual educational possibilities. Certainly here is something to conjure with if man is to understand his place in nature. People raise an eye as if I were a bit loose in the head when I get on the subject of homology and morphology in the orchid flower. Well, be that as it may, we have just about finished two volumes with some 300 colored and detailed drawings that I hope will some day see its way through the presses."

One day he arrived at my office. I had not been expecting him. "Carl Ramsey, your radio friend, has come to see you," said my secretary. I was delighted.

We looked each other over and then shook hands warmly. I had not expected to see a Walt Whitman-like figure, bearded and heavy and well into his seventies. He had the ruddy cheeks and clear eyes that come from living out of doors. In his lively twinkly eyes and gay smile was the making of a Santa Claus.

"What are you doing in New York?" I asked.

"I'm here to address the annual meeting of the American Orchid Society."

I expressed surprise. "I'm a bit surprised too," he said. "I'm not much for speech-making or academics or high society. I'm a self-taught naturalist, have read everything I can get my hands on, but most of what I know I've got from living close to nature, observing and studying. It's been my life. I spend a lot of time and thought raising orchids. In my lecture I hope to show slides of some of mv beauties."

I confessed that I knew nothing about orchids.

"In my reading," said my guest, "I came across a fascinating book by Charles Darwin, *The Fertilization of Orchids by Insects.* This was

many years ago. It became a sort of bible for me. I carried it everywhere in my briefcase. On one page Darwin described a particular
orchid, the Star Orchid of Madagascar. A minister, the Reverend
William Ellis, had sent some of these orchids to England in 1854.
Darwin wrote that this orchid bloomed only at night. How could a
night-blooming orchid be pollinated? Darwin said it had to be by a
night insect, a moth. And how would the moth be attracted? By the
beautiful fragrance of the nectar of the flower. But this orchid had a
long stem and long petals. The moth would be attracted by the
fragrance of the nectar at the base, but it would have to have a long
tongue or proboscis to be able to reach down. Where was I to see this
Star Orchid? And where was I ever to see for myself this unusual
moth? The subject intrigued me. I began to read and carried on a
correspondence with scientists in Madagascar and England and other
parts of the world."

"Have you actually had evidence of this orchid and the moth?" I
asked.

"It took time; years elapsed. I'd almost given up; then one cold
afternoon in January 1929, while I was walking with my little
daughter in Prospect Park, Brooklyn, we decided to warm up in the
nearby greenhouse. When we came to the entrance, my eyes quickly
swept the area. Of all the romance in an unromantic spot! There,
from the glass roof hung the Star, a six-pointed snow-white star!"

Carl explained that the gardener and "Commissioner" of the
Botanical Gardens gave him permission to take one of the orchids for
dissection. He continued: "That same evening, even though it was

severed from the plant, promptly at 6:30 P.M. the fragrance of the orchid came on—stronger and stronger until our apartment was heavy with the lotus-like perfume. I was intoxicated with the flower's performance and slept little that night."

Our friendship continued. Then one day he called me and asked if I would officiate at his daughter's wedding in Bronxville. It was the second and last time I saw him. Some years later, in 1968, Peggy called me to say that her father had died. Would I come up to Vermont and conduct the funeral on a Sunday afternoon? Carl was being cremated. The ashes, according to his wishes, would be deposited in the swamp he loved.

It was early spring, too early for any warmth or green to show. On a Sunday, cold and gray and heavy with rain, my wife and I drove up to Vermont and found "Swampacres." We met the family at the little house and then proceeded in informal procession to the heart of the swamp. The trees were leafless, wet, and black against the gray sky. While rain poured down from their hats and noses and the few umbrellas which some had thought to bring, friends and neighbors stood on slippery logs or wet rocks and in mud.

I spoke of Carl Ramsey as a man, .a person of keen intelligence and with love of truth, a sensitive spirit attuned to earth and all living things, great and small. I said, "A man can live in a swamp and make it a center of kindness and understanding, as well as a means of penetrating to the secrets of the natural world. He can have a great love for his family and his community and his hopes for a better life for those who live in other lands. He was one of the most honest human beings and one who had a clear sense of the values he was ready to live for and die for."

We stood together in the cold, gray wetness as a grandson placed the canister of ashes in the muddy earth just as Carl wanted it. In silence we walked back to the house and the coffee, with grateful feeling for Carl's life and his friendly affection and love for all of us.

A few days later I received a letter from Edith, Carl's wife.

"Dear Friend: You will never know how grateful I am for the simple Sunday service. The editor of *The Banner* said you talked to each one of us direcdy. The whole setting, even the rain and the birds singing, seemed so fitting to dear Carl—Nature seemed so in accord and everyone had a deep sense of this which your talk heightened. I woke up the next morning feeling the desire to live on, not just exist. There was no crippling sorrow or regret for our life together—just hope that I could do something—I don't know what just now—to justify my life in respect to him. I won't say life with him was easy—I had a lot of adjusting to do—we spent our honeymoon camping. I was a city-bred girl who had never camped out. But he opened up a whole new world to me. We would have been married fifty years in June. . .

Grace

Bill Stone and I had gone to elementary and high school together. Bill's mother, Redelia, was an administrative officer of the Ethical Culture Society.

He and I had hiked and worked on a farm down in south Jersey to help raise crops during the labor shortage of World War I.

Those of us who were friends of Bill could only rejoice when we heard he had married Grace, a fellow student at Reed College. When we met her we knew that she was a delightful and lovely human being, sensitive to all living things, from flowers to people. In

recognition of the quality of her work as a physician, Grace was appointed Clinical Director of the Health . Department (1948—2954) and then Director of Health Services and Assistant to the Director of Public Health in charge of School Health Programs in the District of Columbia.

After many years of married happiness and hard work at her profession and in the community, and having raised a lovely daughter and handsome son, Grace came down with a serious heart condition. When she died, Bill asked me to speak at the memorial service to be held in the Friends Meeting House in Washington, D.C. Present were fellow physicians and school officials, parents and teachers, patients and friends, as well as family and many neighbors. It is impossible to convey the atmosphere

and mood of the historic Quaker Meeting House in the
old section of the nation's capital. We sat together in
silence. After a suitable interval, 1 stood and spoke.

We are all drawn together by our common bond of
respect and admiration, our gratitude and love for Grace Stone.
Some knew her because of her work in the clinics and hospitals and
the medical services for children. Some grew up with her. And some
knew her as friends and neighbors. We all treasured her presence,
her beauty, and her friendship.

She was so quiet and so much alive, so keenly intelligent and
informed and skilled, and at the same time so sensitive to beauty and
whatever is gracious in life. She was serious and concerned about the
suffering of the world, the child in the street, the human being next
door, but she also could smile and laugh gloriously.

Over two thousand years ago Socrates said, "No evil can befall a
good person either in life or after death." Most of her life, no evil
befell her. But at the end she suffered and suffered greatly. Because
she was a physician, more than most she knew what her illness
meant, what she had to go through. But she had the will to live and
work and love as long as there was a possibility. She showed a
capacity to endure, "grace under pressure"—and always with courage
and concern and tenderness for others. She was a giving person and
she gave herself as long as she could.

No one ever achieves perfection. But something about Grace
makes me feel that she came very close to an absolute goodness. She

was one of the most innocent people I have ever known. It was unusual. A child is born innocent. It may be sheltered and kept innocent for some time, knowing neither good nor evil. But Grace was a grown person, adult in the fullest sense of the word. She was not sheltered. She knew good and evil. Hers was the innocence and wisdom of the twice-born. She saw and knew the hurt people do to one another. She could be indignant and denounce evil acts. But she could never feel hatred. It was as if she saw both parties to human conflict as victims. She knew what it meant to be fair and just, to be compassionate and forgiving. There could be no taint of destructiveness or malice in purpose or means of achieving ends. She had a deep trust in life, in others, and in herself. If the words "the pure in heart" have meaning, they surely are true of Grace. She was the pure in heart who knew the tough realities and evils of life but was never diverted or contaminated or corrupted by them. If anything, they spurred her more to give herself for what was honest and loving.

Now, in the quietness which follows death, we carry her love and her hopes in our hearts. May we keep faith with her spirit and treasure her qualities and her purposes and carry on her work as long as we live. I am sure if she could speak to us, she would say with George Eliot:

> I like not only to be loved but also to be told that I
> am loved.
> The realm of silence is large beyond the grave.
> This is the world of light and speech.
> And I shall take leave to tell you that you are very dear.

Benjamin Cohen

Born in Concepcion, Chile, of humble parents, Benjamin Cohen distinguished himself early in life, and rose to the highest ranks of the Chilean diplomatic service. His participation in the foreign service of his country as Ambassador to Bolivia and Venezuela, and his activities in Pan-American Conferences contributed to his expertness in international affairs. After serving as Chief of Section in the Preparatory Commission of the United Nations in London, he held the post of Assistant Secretary General in charge of Public Information, and, later, Under Secretary of the Department of Trusteeship and Information for Non-Self-Governing Territories in the United Nations.

1 first met Ben Cohen when the campers and staff of the Encampment for Citizenship were on a field trip to the United Nations. Through the years of his high office at the United Nations, we could always count on him to arrange for our visit and to make sure that we saw and heard everything that was important. He addressed the campers and held discussions with them, not only at the U.N., but over the many years he visited the Encampment, usually on Sunday evenings.

Often he sat out on the grass with his coat off and
discussed international problems until the wee hours.
j4s our friendship grew, not only did we have many
exchanges concerning the philosophies of Humanism,
but he also felt drawn to the Ethical Movement and
sent his children to the Ethical Culture Schools.

The memorial service was held at the Community
Church on March 15, 1960. Those who participated
in the service were the Honorable Daniel Schweitzer,
Permanent Representative of Chile to the United
Nations, and the Honorable Dag Hammarskjold,
Secretary-General of the United Nations. Dr. Donald
Harrington delivered the opening reading and the
benediction. My remarks follow.

We are gathered here to try to express the admiration and love we feel for Benjamin Cohen. I am sure that every one
of us can speak of him as a friend.

Sometimes a man gives us a gift which he buys with money, and it
is a great pleasure to receive it. Sometimes a man gives us a gift
which he makes with his own hands, with his own design and
imagination, his own skill and energy, and we are even more grateful. But sometimes a man gives us himself, and this is the greatest
gift of all. When he shares our life, the sad and happy moments, the
victories and the defeats, when he lives in our life as well as his own,
then he touches our life with the uniqueness of his own person.

When he does this, he brings out something in us which no one else can evoke. And the more unique he is in his nature and temperament, his rhythms and gifts and viewpoints, the more he brings forth in us untouched aspects of our nature. It is literally true that this man touched the lives of thousands in this personal and unique and evocative way. He gave himself to each of us and by his gift each of us is more of a person. Because of him each of us has more hunger for truth, more integrity, more vision, and more faith. This is a man who taught many of us how to reach our hands out to one another, how to put our arms around one another in hearty embrace. Benjamin Cohen felt and expressed his friendliness for human beings passionately and sincerely. His was never a small narrow world or a world of cold formalities or polite verbalisms. His was the world of the warm heart.

Because of him every one of us has more capacity for affection and love. Each of us is a better person because he lived. And the wonderful thing is that when a man gives us himself, then when he dies we do not lose the gift. It is part of our very selves. We are different because of him, and the gift he gave us will be with us as long as we live. If there is truth and goodness in the way one life can touch other lives and live in the life of others, it is exemplified in the life of this dear, dear friend.

He would like us to remember that he was born in his beloved Chile, that he was born of people of little material means but with a great respect and love for learning and great ambition for their children. From his earliest years he had a love of books and read hungrily. All his life he was a reader and a student. At an early age he had a fine sense of values and a high sense of honor. He once said that he might never bring his family money but he would bring them honor. This be has done.

He would like us to think of him as a worker. He had pride in his profession as a journalist. At various times he was a reporter, correspondent, press attache, writer, and editor. Although he may not have called himself such, he was a natural teacher with a rare gift for communication, for making people think, for enlarging their world. As a lecturer and public speaker he was always stimulating and inspiring. His interest in education was evident in his devoted chairmanship of the Board of Trustees of the United Nations Children's School and his membership on the faculty of one of our colleges. At his death he was editor of the Encyclopedia of the Nations, a project close to his heart. For his many contributions to the betterment of mankind, he was honored by a number of universities.

Few men have ever had more love for their native country than he had. Wherever he lived and worked, he dreamed of Chile, the earth he loved and the people he loved and remembered. He longed to be at rest there. Because of that love he appreciated the honor of serving his people in the foreign service. Whether he served as a secretary or charge d'affaires, or ambassador to other nations or to the United Nations, he gave himself to the work with all his heart and mind.

In his distinguished career he received many awards and citations and honors, but no recognition given him meant as much as the trust and responsibility which his own homeland placed upon his shoulders. By the way he served he brought honor to his nation, his government, and his people. No one did more than he to communicate the spirit of Latin America to the rest of the world. By his personality he did much to break through the prejudice and stereotype and ignorance about the Latin American—he made us all eager to visit his country and to know and enjoy his people and their culture and way of life. The flag of his country covers his casket as a symbol of his love and his high sense of honor.

His devotion to the cause of peace found expression in the United Nations. No man could say with such a full heart, "I am grateful for the idea which has used me. I am grateful for the dream that enlisted my heart and my life."

He brought vitality and humanity to the United Nations. The Charter was a sacred document, as sacred as the Old and New Testament, the Koran and the Bhagavad-Gita. For him the Charter was a holy word, a scripture of the righteousness and compassion and love that were needed if men were to achieve peace.

For Benjamin Cohen, the United Nations was more than the buildings and the Charter and meetings and procedures; for him peace was not merely the absence of war—it was.a way of life. It was men meeting and talking together, adjusting their differences, being reconciled to one another, understanding one another. More than most people he understood the meaning of the word "pluralism"—the manyness of man. He respected and treasured the great diversity of

folkways and languages, the institutions and ideologies of the different nations. He dreamed and worked that the day might come when
there would be a free flow of communication and good will between
all members of the human family.

As Assistant Secretary General for Public Information or as Under
Secretary for Trusteeships and Non-Self-Governing Territories, he
identified with the people down under, with the small nations, with
the non-self-governing peoples, with those who were learning to
stand up as equals with others in the family of mankind. He was
sensitive to the differences of tempo as people moved forward in
history.

In the years to come, as we walk the corridors of the United
Nations, we will always feel that he is walking by our side. In the
international conferences where men share and debate their problems, his understanding and his love and faith will speak forth in
those of us who are enriched by his spirit.

He had a tremendous zest for life and a capacity to enjoy life. He
liked food and drink. He liked to smoke. He loved to talk and laugh.
He had a genius for conversation and companionship. He was rare in
combining a hearty, robust nature with quiet gentleness and sensitivity. He was a tender man and a strong man. In the deepest sense
he was religious, a man with true reverence for life.

Family meant much to him. Family meant the home he was born
in and to which he brought so much honor. It meant devotion to his
sisters. He was a devoted husband to the wife he adored. His children were seldom out of his thoughts. His love and concern for those

nearest and dearest will live on in them—and as he brought honor to them and the name he gave them, so they will bring honor to his memory. The deep happiness he knew with those he loved is evident in these lines from an unidentified Chilean poet, which he often quoted:

> It is the glory of life
> That there are some who
> When we hold them up to the full light of the sun,
> The radiance shines through
> And there are no black spots, no evil.
> So here we celebrate the life of one
> Whose dreams and deeds have brought justice and
> love
> To the lives of all of us.
> Because of him, we are better people,
> Because of him we have hope of a better life.
> He was one who with full heart could say:
> "I have loved,
> I have been loved,
> The sun has caressed my face.
> Life, you owe me nothing
> Life, we are at peace."

Milton Avery

Milton Avery died in 1965. Sally Avery, his wife, called to ask if the memorial service might be held in the Meeting House. Milton Avery was a Protestant by ancestry, but a Humanist in his approach to life. When I called on Mrs. Avery, she met me in the doorway of their home. She said, "Before we sit down to talk, let us walk through the rooms of our apartment. My husband's paintings will reveal more about his philosophy and his life than anything I could say." In silence, we walked through the rooms and stood before treasures of art, treasures of the ways a man had seen life; his approach to reality, with simplicity and beauty.

At the memorial service, the Meeting House was filled with artists who revered Milton Avery, representatives of museums, directors of galleries, critics, officers of art foundations, and many, many friends.

We meet together to honor the life and the work and the memory of a great artist and a great person. Although there is sadness and grief in this room, we take consolation from the fact that Milton Avery lived a long life, a good life, and a creative life—far, far more than most human beings. We like to think that he enjoyed his life—the serenities, the creative moments, the recognition, and the feelings of achievement. He must have known that his work would live on after his death.

Most of all, I think we appreciate that he was true to himself. Emerson said that "A man's obedience to his own genius is faith in its highest form." I like to think of that.

It may be easy to keep faith with one's self when everything is with you, when it's the popular thing to do; it is much harder when you are a nonconformist or an innovator and a spirit moved by unique originality. There were hard years, many hard years, for Milton Avery and for his wife. There wasn't much money. What there was might have gone to make life easier, more comfortable. But art can demand sacrifices. And Milton permitted nothing to divert or distract him from the thing he most wanted to do: to paint what he saw and what he felt, to communicate it. This was his passion, his devotion. He was faithful to himself, faithful to the people closest to him, and faithful to an ideal.

We think not only of Milton Avery but of his wife, Sally, who through all the years shared his life in so many ways and made the paintings possible. We owe her a great debt.

For so long a time we Americans drew on Europe and had no time for or interest in our own original creative potential. As I was listening to the music, I was thinking of so much that has happened in the last half-century in this country—in the last twenty years and the last forty years. The American people have learned; and have become more and more responsive and supportive to what amounts in the larger sense to the development of American culture, American civilization, and with it the enrichment of the civilization of man. We are more than just a nation of factories and production lines; much more than gadgets and supermarkets in the people we will bring forth. So, I am speaking not only of his contribution to art, which will live as the generations pass, but of what is also noble and heroic—to lift man up in his sense of what he is, to lift man up in his faith in what he can be.

The wonderful thing the great artist does for us is to help us see life with more wonder and understanding, to see and feel and sense the beauty that we never saw before. This is a spiritual gift, a pure thing. At least, this is what the paintings say to me. Everyone who knew him and knows his work is a better person because he lived and created. Everyone who understood him has more sensitivity, more courage, more devotion, more faith in the values of the human—aesthetic and moral. The wonderful thing is that when he dies, we do not lose what he gave us. It becomes part of our life. This is true of him as a dear husband and father, a dear friend and fellow artist. He lives in those he loves. He lives in his creations. He lives as he gives himself to his age and to his world. I have here a letter written by Wallace Putnam, a close friend. In 1925 these two artists came to New York from Hartford. Thirty-five years later Wallace wrote the following letter to his seriously ill friend, Milton Avery.

"I think of you as one of the most extraordinary men I know. From the beginning you seem to have known how to dare and how to trust. You have not had to try and find the answers as I have had to try, hunting in all the books and all the religions for a way of life. Finally, I have come around to realizing that there are no answers to the questions we ask. Our questions have no relation to the reality of life, like questions on how to paint. Finally, we have to give them up and just paint, relying completely on our sense of form, our feelings for relationships. So, in living, I have come to think we have to give up questions about how and why, and trust completely to an inner sense of rhythm. As each touch of paint on canvas has to be felt, has to come from a source of life, a feeling for order deep within us, so every step we take must come from some deep part of us, some self in us that does not doubt and question. Already I am talking too much, what I am trying to say is you, more than anyone I know, seemed to know from the beginning how to dare to put paint on canvas, trusting not in your personal mind and will but trusting in life, two lives, to your brush, to your whole self. And the beauties that have come from your brush teach me and have taught many others what men most need to know, the necessity of daring to trust to life, God, self or whatever it is called. Trusting to this minute, to show us the next step ahead."

May it be said of us, as we now say: he was loved in his life, and he has left undying love behind him at his death. May his memory, his sensitivity, his intelligence, his serenity, his courage, and his faith be with us until the end of our days.

I conclude our service with the words of Santayana:

With you a part of me has passed away.
For in the peopled forest of my mind,
A tree made lifeless by this wintry wind
Shall never don again its green array.
Chapel and fireside, country road and bay
Have something of their friendliness resigned.
Another, if I would, I could not find,
And I am grown much older in a day.
And yet I treasure in my memory your gifts, your
  young heart's ease.
For these once mine, my life is rich with ease.
And I scarce know which part greater be,
What I keep of you or what you robbed from me.

Harry Brandt

Through the years, the children and grandchildren,
nieces and nephews of the Brandt family were
students
at the Ethical Culture Schools. As a teacher, I had
them in my classes. Knowing the children meant
knowing the parents, and that meant knowing the
family and, above all, Harry. Our personal relationship
grew because of a common interest in the field of civil
rights, and especially the abolition of discrimination in

housing, through the New York State and National
Committees. Harry Brandt had been the head of the
Independent Movie Theater Owners' Association. He
was an officer of the Trans-Lux Corporation. But his
office walls were covered with awards and tributes
from the many organizations he had helped in their
work for better education, health, and welfare.
Although he was not a member of the Ethical Culture
Society, he contributed generously to the Scholarship
Fund of the Ethical Culture Schools. 1 made the
following remarks at his funeral service.

Every human life is precious, every human life in
the world. But for each of us a few lives are precious beyond all
others. They are the lives of those who are close in family, in work,
in neighborliness. Such was the life of Harry Brandt. He was
unusually close to many people and much beloved. Our presence
here is evidence of our common bond through his life.

We lose those we love. There is no way out of it. Death is part of
life. Even when we know and accept the fact as part of a mature
philosophy of life, we are never quite completely accepting of it
when it occurs. This is shock. There is need for time to make
adjustment.

Deeper is the pain of parting. In the linkage of life with life, the
more we love each other, the more we suffer the loss. Our roots go
deep into each other's heart. But we should not be afraid to love for

fear that some day we will be hurt. We give our love trustfully and generously as long as we can have each other. So it is in marriage, and between parents and children and friends.

Harry Brandt was a hearty man, a warmhearted human who could never greet you formally or coldly, but always with a tremendous smile and a warm embrace. He loved life and people. He would be the first to say, "Don't grieve. I had a long life and a good life, lots of fulfillment and many reasons for being grateful."

In keeping with his spirit we should celebrate his life. He would have liked it that way.

It is fitting that we are gathered at this Meeting House of the Ethical Society. The Brandt family has sent its children and grand-children, its nieces and nephews, to the Ethical Culture Schools, and some of us have had the pleasure of enjoying them in our classes. Besides, some of us have worked with Harry Brandt to try to solve a number of important human needs in the community, and have had close friendships with him and members of the family. Harry was close to the Ethical Movement, though not a member of it. He was clear about his identity—far more than most people. He knew he was a Jew by ancestry and had a feeling of identity with the Jewish community. He was proud of his ancestry, the history of the people he came from, their capacity to survive extreme persecution and their capacity to make creative contributions to civilization and the com-mon life. He was also an. American identified with this nation, its institutions, its heritage and its way of life. He was aware of his larger identity with the human race. And he showed it by the reach of his associations and the ideas and ideals which engaged his interest and motivated him for human betterment.

Harry Brandt had good reason to rejoice in his family and especially his marriage. It meant a long-time love with companionship and sharing, each assuring the other security and effectiveness, each proud of and enjoying the other's accomplishments. And we are grateful to Harry's wife for making possible the kind of life he lived, a home for a family and children, a home from which a man could go forth to work and act in the community. The Brandt family is large, but its members are close and warm in feelings about each other. People have stood by each other. The family has enjoyed and shared with one another. They have been involved in business together— not always easy, a good test.

Through all the years Harry Brandt has been remarkable in his energy, his persistence, his devotion to the theater and the world of showmanship—the exciting and challenging and changing world of motion pictures. In his life great changes have taken place—from silent movies, "talkies'," color pictures, and on into television—and beyond all that the outreach from local and domestic to foreign films and then the growing awareness that the films must be considered not merely as a technical matter or a business or entertainment, but as an art. Through all those changes in a highly competitive field where business has to earn its way day by day, Harry worked intelligently, shrewdly, and with imagination and humanity.

He had the optimism and the sportsmanship at its best of a gambler. The theater is a gamble. He took risks, staked on what he thought worth investing in. If it did not work out and he lost, he began again, never defeated. He enjoyed that side of life—the game part of it.

But the thing that impressed many of us most was that he worked out so much of himself in a difficult and precarious area of the city, Times Square. A man can walk through dirt and not be dirtied. A man can walk through surroundings of bad taste and keep his standards. A man can walk through corruption and not be corrupted by it. A man can be exposed to bigotry and not become bigoted. And a man can move through a confusion of values and not lose his sense of what is important, the values of highest priority. It's easy if we move in sheltered, refined, elite circles. But Times Square is tough and sometimes it is all the things a man should stay away from. I see him walking and working there for what he believed, and preserving and growing in his sense of what was decent. He didn't just survive or exploit the situation. He lived for what he believed in; against the noise and glitter and corruption and bigotry, he came out a human being.

Some of us were in his office often, usually when there was trouble or injustice or someone needing help. When we called, he would say, "Come down and lunch with me." We would eat at his desk. All around on the walls were the tributes and awards and medals, expressions of appreciation from religious and racial groups, professional organizations, civic movements—the United Jewish Appeal, Catholic Charities, the Wiltwyck School for Boys, Red Cross, Police Athletic League, March of Dimes—there was no end to them. To each and all he brought imagination, energy, effort. It was part of his citizenship, part of his sense of building a community. He was a man of compassion. He listened. He was generous. He wanted to help. It was part of his nature. He had a kind heart. He liked to build bridges between people who were different and differed. Whether it was the Cardinal and Eleanor Roosevelt or the Mayor and his critics, Harry Brandt was there trying to help.

I have one particular experience I would like to share with you. Before the civil rights movement was popular, back in 1950, he came to a luncheon of a dozen people at the invitation of Eleanor Roosevelt. The purpose was to launch the National Committee Against Discrimination in Housing. Mrs. Roosevelt welcomed her wealthy liberal guests. Our goal was research, education, and legislative programs for equal housing opportunity for all Americans. Mrs. Roosevelt asked each guest to say what he thought and what he would give. Harry Brandt was the last. He said, "I won't give you money at this time. I am overcommitted. But I give you thirty thousand tickets to the Trans-Lux movie theaters. You can sell them for fifty cents apiece. If you sell them all, you will have fifteen thousand dollars."

At the time we had no inkling of what he was doing. In the years that followed, these tickets were bought by the thousands by members of the International Ladies' Garment Workers Union, the National Association for the Advancement of Colored People, the tenants of public housing, and the members of agencies and business firms. But the greatest gift was this: in selling the tickets, we had to explain what we were doing, our purposes and our methods. This resulted in a vast educational campaign to sell the idea of Freedom of Residence and Fair Housing Opportunity to tens of thousands of Americans. Each year for years, it meant substantial financial support for the work of the National Committee and the New York State Committee against Discrimination in Housing. It made it possible to carry on educational and legislative campaigns in New York State and also in New Jersey, Connecticut, Rhode Island, and Colorado. The Executive Order on housing aided by federal programs and eventually the Open Housing Law of the federal government were due in part to the support which came from this man. The outreach of this man made a difference and gave hope for a truer democracy for this nation in the years to come.

This man knew how to work and how to share and how to laugh. We are all different and better human beings because he lived. If Harry Brandt were able to speak to us, his beloved family and his beloved community of friends, he would wish us strength and direction and faith for the days to come.

We honor and are grateful to this human being who moved among us with decency and compassion and love. May his influence and his image and his memory be with us in strength and creativeness and courage and love all the rest of our years.

A Double Funeral

The news headline read: AUTO DEALER AND HIS WIFE SLAIN IN CENTRAL PARK WEST ROBBERY. Both were found in their Park West Village apartment with their mouths stuffed with paper and taped, and their throats cut. He was white, Jewish, born in Austria. His wife, black, Protestant. She had two grown children by a former marriage. They had been adopted and loved as his own by the husband. The son and the daughter were students in their middle twenties. The son called me to ask if I would conduct the funeral service for his parents. Why had he called? His father had often listened and spoken about the radio broadcasts of the Sunday morning services of the Ethical Culture Society.

The son, the son's fiancee, and the daughter met with me in my apartment that evening. The daughter said, "I have never seen, and will probably never again know, such a truly happy marriage. My parents were proud of one another. They enjoyed each other twenty-four hours a day. They loved each other and showed it in a thousand different ways. My father's feeling for my mother, and for both of us, was so strong that nothing else mattered. Whatever happened in the outside world, it just didn't matter, compared with the importance of the family. My father was a strong man. He knew what he was doing, whether it was in business or in his home. In my earlier years I didn't question anything. I trusted and depended on him absolutely. In recent years, if I had any questions, all I know is that whatever my father did or didn't do, he did it for the family. Family was every- thing to him."

When I questioned the son, he said, "When my father married my mother, his family didn't accept the marriage. He lost some of his white friends. He felt he was deserted and betrayed. If you ask me, "Who were my father's friends?' I have to say that most of his friends were black."

At the chapel, I walked out to stand by the two coffins and face approximately a hundred and fifty people, five of whom were white. What struck me was the fact that those present formed one of the most interesting and intelligent and attractive groups of people I have ever faced. Some faces showed genuine grief. But most were impassive. It was as if they had learned to suppress any outward expression of such a thing as grief. At least this was my impression.

Perhaps it was this lack of outward expression that moved me to say: "Whatever the differences in our backgrounds, we are drawn together by the tragedy of these two deaths. This husband and wife loved each other. For twelve years they shared life and made a good home and loved their children. Many of you know them as friends and neighbors. Many of you know them as business associates. I did not know them. But I have come to know them through discussions with their children—their marriage, their home life, their life with their son and their daughter. I have something of a sense of the business in which they all worked together.

"I am sure that we all are grown up enough and realistic enough to know that we all die, and we will all lose those we love. Our problem is not to fear death, but to live without fear and overcome fear, so that we can live effectively and creatively and lovingly. I have strong feelings about the circumstances of this death, this double death, this double murder, I cannot help speaking of it here and now. It seems to me that the dead would want me to do so.

"When someone dies, someone we love, the anguish is great, no matter what the cause. Natural forces beyond the control of human beings—an earthquake, a flood, a volcano—can kill those we love. When it happens because of human carelessness or human weakness, we may suffer even more, because it strikes us that the death was so unnecessary and useless. If the death is caused by human beings because of hate or anger or greed, the loss is just as great. But in this case, we are bound to have a feeling of great sorrow and tragedy. In such a case, it is society which has to pass the judgment. For an intentional and deliberate and premeditated killing is far worse than a death resulting from self-defense or anger or carelessness. This is the worst kind of human action. This is not just against individuals, people we love; it is an action against society itself, against all of us. And this was intentional, deliberate, planned, and premeditated. It was a double killing, the murder of a husband and* wife in a home, and in a happy marriage. And whether it was done by those who wanted to kill, or whether they hired others to do the double murder, this is the worst of all—a cruel, brutal act, an act of absolute evil."

On the way to the cemetery, I wondered: Could this have been a murder due to the fact of an interracial marriage? No, not in New York City in 1972. Could it have been motivated by robbery? No, there was no evidence that anything had been taken from the apartment or the persons of the dead. Could the double murder be traced to something that happened in' Europe in the days of Hitler's Nazism: the domination and aggression and collaboration of underground resistance movements? True, he had been an officer of the underground resistance movement. But if this were so, why kill his wife?

At the cemetery, photographers from the newspapers or from the police, I could not tell which, were stationed at the entrance. They took films of all of us while we were still in the cars, and later standing at the grave. At the double grave, standing before the very expensive coffins covered with many flowers, I faced about fifty of the people who had attended the services at the chapel in the city. Of the fifty, five were white. Two were plainclothesmen. I spoke the final words.

"Each of us has very little time on this earth, just a few years. We walk about, and work, and love, and seek happiness. Just as we have a limited number of years, so we have a limited space. How much can a body take up—six feet tall, the reach of our arms? When we think of the size of the earth and outer space, each of us is very small, in the air we displace and the weight as we walk about and love. At death, we return the body to the earth. We are creatures of earth, and we give back to earth that which was of earthly origin. What, then, remains? We live a life of productivity and creativity and love. We reach out to others. We extend our spirit far beyond our bodies. And so each of us in time and space is far more than we seem. We are more than the space we occupy in life, and the earth we occupy in death.

"Standing here at the grave of these two dear people, who were faithful in their love and their lives together, we who are closest in friendship and family have accompanied them at the end and wish to express our respect and admiration and affection. We are grateful they shared their lives with us, thankful for the years they gave us, for the support and nourishment and friendship.

"In this place hallowed by their memory, green grass will flourish, and the flowers will bloom each spring with color and fragrance and new life. So may it be in the years to come, that each of us has a sense of regeneration of life. May we leave this place not in despair and sorrow, but in the spirit of their trust and courage and their way of facing life. May we always feel their presence in moments of great joy, and in moments also when we need strength and courage. I hope we will never forget them: what they have meant to us and will mean to us in life and in death."

Funeral of a Freedom Fighter

Some years after World War II, an outstanding leader of the Hungarian underground resistance movement died in New York City. He had grappled for years with occupation forces of the Nazis and the Soviet Union in Hungary. His widow and grown sons were in a quandary. They had followed his wish that he be cremated at death. But the widow said that he had not believed in ceremonies, and least of all in funeral and memorial services. Indeed, he had never attended a funeral service during his life. None of the family were traditionally religious, but many of the friends—and there were many—thought that something was needed. They felt that they could not just bury a man's body in the earth or burn him to ashes, and then go their separate ways. One friend suggested that it might be appropriate to hold a memorial service at the Ethical Society.

The room we had set aside at the Ethical Society could seat fifty or sixty persons. Between one hundred and one hundred and fifty persons crowded the outer edges and flowed out into the hall. I welcomed those who were present: "We have gathered to try to express our respect and admiration, our gratitude and affection, for a great human being. He was a person of gifts. He was a man of character. We know him as a husband in a marriage which through many years has been an expression of true love and companionship. We know him as a citizen completely dedicated to freedom and equality, and as a man of courage who would stand and resist and fight for what he believed and who was ready to pay with his life for his values and convictions. We know him as a strong man devoted to the welfare and development of his sons. We know him as one who tried to help wherever people were in trouble. What he spoke he tried to live by. He did so more than most of us.

"I shall call on two friends to speak and then ask if anyone present would like to share with us what he meant in your life. Would you please stand up and say, 'How I remember him'?"

The first friend had shared the struggles and the dangers and the imprisonment. The second gave his thoughts in Esperanto, but preceded his statement with an explanation and interpretation in English. When I invited people to speak, a man stood up and spoke in his native Hungarian. Then a little elderly woman stood up and opened her purse and said, "I have written a poem in honor of our beloved brave man. May I read it?" She was not a great poet, but it was a lovely tribute. Then a tall young woman, blond and attractive, walked forward to the front of the room. "I'd like to say a word to the younger generation. This man, with all that he had lived through and fought for, was one of the older generation who understood youth. I, for one, never met a person in public life who inspired such trust. For me and many of my generation his life and his character are an unforgettable symbol of faith."

The quality of feeling among the people cannot adequately be put into words. Who could possibly interpret the many sad and tragic memories of those present? So many of the Hungarian community were indebted to him for their lives and their hopes and their very faith in life and the future.

A few years later I met with one of the sons. I asked whether he had any recollection of the memorial service for his father. He said, "He never believed in funerals. We as a family were quite ready to follow his way of thinking. But my mother was in great distress, and a friend said that my father would have felt at home with the kind of nondogmatic and nonsectarian Humanism which is the Humanism of the Ethical Movement."

I asked what the service had meant to him. He said, "Frankly, I didn't have a very positive attitude. But it was just right for the family. If I may say it, that memorial service not only was in keeping with my father's spirit, but it 'wrapped up' his death. It helped us face the fact that this was the end of his life. It helped us pull ourselves together and start our life in the future without him. Besides this, it afforded us a tremendous feeling of release and relief."

Tribute to
Martin Luther King Jr.

A Jazz Requiem

(One year after his assassination: April 6, 1969)

The Requiem, composed and conducted by Ronald Roullier, was performed by the New York Jazz Repertory Orchestra and the New York Group Singers, directed by Jack Manno, with James Earl Jones as narrator, at the Meeting House of the New York Society for Ethical Culture. The auditorium was overflowing and through loudspeakers hundreds heard

the program in other rooms of the Society and in the
street. Those present had a hard time maintaining the
silence appropriate to a requiem. Heads nodded, feet
tapped, hands clapped, and the pent-up response at
the end was a standing ovation for the composer, the
musicians, and Mr. Jones. It was a glorious morning of
tribute to a great human being. The entire program was
conceived and produced by David G. Black, theater
producer. The narration was my work. The music set
the mood and expressed beautifully the spirit of the
narration.

FREE AT LAST
Today we celebrate a man and a life,
We pay tribute to Martin Luther King,
Spiritual leader and a leader of men, a leader in the
nation, a world of human freedom and peace.

BOY TO MAN
Martin Luther King, Jr., was born in Atlanta, Georgia,
    January 15, 1929.
Reared in Georgia and Alabama,
He knew the shacks of the southland, the life of the
    sharecroppers, and the ministry.

As a boy-child in Alabama he knew the evils of op-
   pression and the rejection of racism.
Jim Crow forced him behind a curtain in a railroad car.
Jim Crow drove him to the back of the bus.
The Cross, perverted to evil use, was burned as a
   weapon of terror by men who hid behind the
   hoods of the Klan.
He saw the fear and the hate around him.
A boy may play in a world of his own,
A world where neighbors walk hand in hand.
But the day comes when he finds doors closed by his
   own playmates,
His playmates' parents saying,
"Play with your own kind.
That black boy is off limits."
Rejection can break a boy or make him strong
   And the boy becomes a man with hot anger against injustice,
With a will to strike out against evil
   And a deep hunger for brotherhood.
The *boy-child-becomes-a-man,* studies at Morehouse
   College and Boston Theological.
Like his grandfather and his father before him he is
   ordained and preaches in the church which his
   ancestors had served.

YOUNG MAN'S DREAM

Martin Luther King, Jr., came out of a small world
  with a dream
  And his world grew and his dream grew—
The man believed in the freedom-dream of the old world,
He believed in the promise of freedom in the new world,
And he made the dream his own.
He walked to the rhythm of the dream,
Made it a marching song out of his own heartbeat
With its own melody and its own syncopation of
  freedom and a new life not just for himself and
  black people—for all people.
And those who heard it, black and white, moved to
  its beat and rhythm with singing hearts—they
  heard it and they marched.

He speaks and his voice is resonant with the beat
  and harmony of the freedom dream—the hungers
  and longings of the oppressed of the nation—the
  oppressed of the earth.
And the voice carries far and wide.

BUS RIDE

On an afternoon in 1955
Rosa Parks was returning home from work.

The bus driver said, "Get to the back of the bus."
Rosa Parks was tired,
Tired of being ordered about and humiliated,
Tired of giving up her seat to a white man.
She kept her seat. She would not be moved.
And when they arrested her, the black people of
   Montgomery waited.
Who would speak? Who would give the word?

Martin Luther King, Jr., was a minister young in
   years,
He was a leader above all factions, and he called for
   the bus boycott.
"It is better to walk in dignity
Than to ride in Humiliation."

The racists said, "The nigras will not walk."
The racists said, "It will rain. The nigras will not walk."
But the people walked.
Old and young, they walked miles and miles for
   weeks and weeks
   And the buses ran empty.
There was harassment and persecution
   But the people persisted
   And the powers had to yield.

LET FREEDOM RING
   Freedom!
A long hard road,
For while many cried, "Freedom now! Freedom
   now!"
Those who feared and hated,
Those who were blind
Resisted, saying, "Not yet! Not Yet! What do they
   want?"
And others cried, "Never! Never!"
Bombs wrecking his home,
Jails and threats of assassination
   Did not turn him back.
He would not be turned aside, he could not be
   denied
And the people turned to him.

Where there was fear he taught courage,
Where there was cruelty he taught compassion,
   Where there was hate he taught love,
And where there was violence he taught the ways of
   peace.
   He was a preacher and a Freedom Man.

Freedom! A new self, a new courage, a commitment.
  To be tested in the hot fires of power conflict,
Tested in the factions and division of his own people,
  Reviled and rejected and threatened with death,
  And still the man stood
  And his voice rang out, "Let Freedom Ring!"
And the people sang, "Let Freedom Ring!"
Through the length and breadth of the land.

MARCH ON WASHINGTON

In the Second World War,
In the time of Franklin Roosevelt
  The *threat* of a March on Washington
  Brought forth the President's Executive Order for
  Fair Employment Practices.
Now in 1963 in the time of John Kennedy, the
  March on Washington became a reality.

The skeptics said, "It will never come to pass,
The people will not come.
There is apathy and fear."
The timid said, "There will be violence and blood-
  shed!"

But the word went forth throughout the nation.
By bus and train, by car and plane,
Black and white, rich and poor, they came from
    every state,
North and South, East and West
    Hand in hand, banners streaming,
Talking, laughing, singing,
Walking in the sun, walking in the quiet silence
    of friends,
A quarter of a million Americans walking in the na-
    tion's capital
From Washington Monument to the Lincoln Memorial.

There were no guns that day
    It was a day to remember
    A day of peace.

I HAVE A DREAM

    There from the high rostrum Martin Luther King spoke: "I have a dream that one day men will rise up and come to see that they are made to live together as brothers. I still have a dream . . . everyone will be judged on the basis of the content of his character rather than the color of his skin, and every man will respect the dignity and worth of human personality . . . one day war will come to an end, that men will beat their swords into plowshares and their spears into pruning hooks, that nation will no longer rise up against nation, neither will they study war any more."

MEMPHIS IN APRIL
Through the centuries, in many lands
Many have died for freedom.
Here! In the American Revolution, the slave
   revolts, the Civil War,
Many have been lynched,
Many have died from the assassin's bullet—too
   many.

It takes years to bring forth heroic Freedom
   Fighters,
It takes just a second to tear apart the human heart
   or brain
Of an Abe Lincoln, a John Kennedy, a Robert
   Kennedy, a Malcolm X, a Martin Luther King.
He survived Montgomery bombs
And the jails of Bull Connors and the handcuffs of
   Jim Clark
   —they could not stop him
He survived the boycotts and marches and sit-ins
   of Birmingham and Chicago and Selma
   —they could not tire him
What drew him? Fate? His heart and love of man?

The meek and the poor were standing up in
   Memphis.
They must not stand alone.

Memphis in April is beautiful with the fragrance of
   flowers
But that April the air was full of death.
In the heavens
The sun hid
From the man-fear and the man-hate,
The freedom-fear and the freedom-hate.

MULE CORTEGE

On April 4th, 1968,
On the balcony of the Lorraine Motel in Memphis,
   Tennessee,
Martin Luther King, Jr., was done to death
And the mule cortege drew the farm wagon
That carried him on the road he had walked all his
   life.
The nations which had honored him with the Nobel
   Peace Prize
Shared the mourning.
It was more than tragedy for those close in his love,

His wife and his parents and his children,
More than tragedy for the black people,
It was tragedy for the world of men—
For all the people of the earth.

WHICH SIDE ARE YOU ON?
There comes a day when a man must face his dream:
   Where does he stand? What should he do? What
   burdens must he carry?
What sacrifices must he make?
And he went up into the mountain
From the darkness of the land,
From the valley of broken promises,
He raised his eyes to a vision of a new nation,
He looked over Jordan into the Promised Land.

We have to ask ourselves
Where do *we* stand? What do *we* believe? What are
   the First Things?
Shall we turn away? The gods are calling the roll.
Will we stand and answer?
Will we act?
Which side?—Which side are you on?

PROMISED LAND

The land brings forth its young,
The land brings forth the promise of freedom,
The hope of equality,
The faith in the human community.

Martin Luther King would say,
"I have been to the mountain
A mountain peak lifting men's eyes
Out over the life of the earth planet,
Over the march of the generations through history.
We have looked out from the mountain,
We have glimpsed the Promised Land.
Even if I never set foot on the sacred soil
I know that *we* are on our way."

FREE AT LAST

Yes, a man may be born to carry a dream on a long
    hard road,
He may march into the presence of his enemies—
    without a sword—
And they may slay him,
But the dream lives
And mankind lives.
Even in death there is Victory!

And the time comes when men can say,
"Free at last!"

John Lovejoy Elliott:
The Way a Man Died

We gathered outside his hospital room. All of us, family, friends, colleagues of the Ethical Culture Society, and social workers of Hudson Guild Settlement. We had heard he was ill. Now we were told his condition was critical. The doctor said it was pneumonia; he was in an oxygen tent. We could see him. Could he see us? Yes, in certain moments when he could open his eyes and pierce through the haze of his own fever and the medication. But even then he did not seem to see us or know us. There came a moment when he tried to peer through the oxygen-tent window and the door. He made some sign which the orderly understood. A paper and pencil were passed in to him. His bed was raised so that he was able to sit up. He wrote something on the paper and then fell back. The bed was lowered. The door was closed.

We talked with one another in the hospital corridor. After about half an hour, the doctor approached. "It's all over," he said very quietly. He handed us the paper with the penciled message scrawled: "The only thing I have known in life worth living and dying for is Love and Friendship."

Much of his work had been in the tenement houses and slum areas of the great city, with people of many colors and creeds, with young and old, rich and poor. His compassion and love knew no bounds. He was the good neighbor in the midst of the busy, competitive, acquisitive city. Many whom he loved and served in the slums of Hell's Kitchen had thought of him as a priest even though he would have nothing of creeds and dogmas, of supernatural affirmations or sectarian divisions. Most people knew him as "Doc L" but many of the devout thought and spoke of him as "Father Elliott."

Before the memorial service at the Meeting House of the Ethical Society, a priest of the local church in Chelsea came to pay his respects.

"Where are the remains?" he asked.

I said, "There are no remains. He was cremated, according to his desire."

"Well, then," said the priest, "he did not believe in the resurrection of the dead?"

"No. He did not believe in an afterlife. But he believed in the brotherhood of man."

"Did he believe in the fatherhood of God?" asked the priest.

"No, he did not believe in the fatherhood of God."

"Well, if he didn't believe in the fatherhood of God, how could he believe in the brotherhood of man?"

"The fact is that he not only believed in the brotherhood of man but taught it and lived it all the years of his life. He did not believe that the brotherhood of man depended on a belief in the fatherhood of God."

"Did he believe in immortality?"

"No. But he believed that a person lived on in the lives of others, in the influence and in the work he had done. He believed that a person lives in the way he touches life and that the good lives through the living. He felt no need for personal immortality."

There Comes a Time

"There comes at some time for each of us the final break when the voice we loved never speaks again, when there is no response from the source that before had never failed us. But we discover that a wonderful thing can happen. Though the physical presence has gone, we need not let the relationship end.

"Our memories are something like dreams, but they are real too. Our hopes are something like dreams, but not all dreams. We who remember, who have worked together, we are held in the bond of memory of the years, held in the hope of a better future. Out of memories and hopes, out of faith in each other, out of what we have learned, we gain the understanding to recognize the things that ought to be supported by us with fullest power.

"There is this new revelation—the revelation of the untapped potentialities of finer life in the human beings we know. Perhaps we have always tended to feel it in those we have lost. We come to know a person in the quietness that follows death; after the storm of grief has passed, a vision of the personality remains. At times, someone with a touch of genius writes an epitaph to testify to the significance of a man dead and gone. But the essence of life is not in epitaphs: it is in living."

—From the thought of John Lovejoy Elliott

INVOCATIONS

Introduction

In the world of primitive societies, and in the ancient world and even in the modern world, it has always been the custom of human beings to offer invocations, calling upon divine powers to protect and assure success in human undertakings. They have offered prayers and incantations, chants and dances, and sacrifices. They have entreated and pleaded. They have called upon the spirits to be present, to protect and shield them, to intercede for them against the forces of evil.

Some of these invocations were offered at times of the year when people were going off on hunting or fishing expeditions. They wanted a calm sea, smooth waters for their boats, or a cloudless sky and warm sun for planting, fertility for their crops and their cattle— or they invoked the unknown powers to bring them many children. Some would invoke the gods for rice and yams, for slaves and riches. They pleaded that they might survive the cold of winter. They invoked the spirits to make them a strong people. When they felt threatened by the powers of nature, an earthquake or a volcano; when storms and floods or drought and plague destroyed life they were crying out for a miracle, for the intercession of spirits to save them.

So also in the modern world, when human beings undertake something which concerns all, even where men practice modern science and know more about the natural world and cause and effect of events, men call upon the supernatural for protection and support.

When we launch a ship; when sailors and soldiers and pilots take off on a dangerous journey; when we achieve something together; when the last tile on the roof or the last beam or the last finishing touch has been completed, we hold a "topping" ceremony for a building. When men take off into outer space, we invoke the gods' power.

In modern society, invocations by clergy may ask a blessing on special occasions or at a worship service. These are appropriate in their separate human gatherings. But even where human beings are united in their belief in monotheism, invocations offered by clergy-men of any one sect may be inappropriate and embarrassing. In community gatherings of mutual concern to people of many different religious traditions, and often including many of the unchurched, if there is to be any invocation at all, it should be inclusive, "beyond sectarianism." Those who are concerned to respect the beliefs and identifications of a great variety of people when the community gathers together seek a common denominator. It is an increasing practice to call for an invocation, or "opening word," expressive of a respect and inclusive humanism and concern for shared values.

Humanist invocations are inclusive and beyond sectarianism. They are not addressed to powers outside man. Each invocation is appro-priate to the specific situation which calls it into being. An invocation may be offered at the beginning of a gathering or it may serve as "closing words" to restate the intent and common purpose and commitment of the occasion. In the following pages are invocations I have spoken on special occasions, and also some which I have used for the opening words or the closing words at meetings of the

Ethical Culture Societies and annual meetings of the American Ethical Union. If they have anything in common, it is that they are not set rituals, they are not repetitious. There is no effort to invoke a magic or a miracle from powers outside of man, but rather to stress human responsibility for the quality of life we want to take and lead.

They are an effort to stimulate consciousness of self and others, consciousness of unity and community, a commitment to the struggle for a better life. The emphasis is not, "O Lord, save us," but "May we take responsibility for the quality of our life, solve our problems together, live up to whatever we hold in the way of human values and the vision of what life might be."

Sunday Meetings

The following invocations have been offered at Sunday morning meetings of the Ethical Culture Societies.

We meet in the tradition of freedom
And the promise of human equality
We call upon ourselves as citizens
To give strength
To the heritage and to fulfill the promise.

We invoke
Those elements of the human spirit
That dignify and ennoble human life.
May our minds be filled
With the wonder of the universe,
The grandeur of the heavens,
And the riches of earth,
The miracle and the mystery
Of human personality.

May our hearts be filled with good will
And our understanding go beyond
The barriers of the past
To a true comradeship with one another.
May the good in every man and woman and
child
Be honored and his rights protected
Regardless of color or creed,
National origin or economic circumstances,

And, may our nation with every year
Grow more fair and just,
A force for peace
In the community of mankind
For our children's sake.

Every day
The rivers flow
Carrying millions of tons
Of precious earth
To the sea.

Every day
Millions
Go to their graves
Without ever having lived
Without knowing love,
Their talents unborn—
Wasted.

   We cannot make men live or want to live. But we can create the conditions in which they will have more taste for life and more faith in life.

   We cannot make men free if they do not want to be free. But we can remove the obstacles to their freedom and help them learn to free themselves.

   We cannot make men equal when they are unequal. But we can help defend their rights and open opportunities that each may follow his interests and develop his talents, and become what he has it in him to be.

   We cannot make men like one another or love one another. But we can reach out to others and help men communicate and understand each other. We can nourish the feeling of community, the feeling of identity in the common life. We can seek to create a climate of trust and good will with those whose lives we touch. This is the way to freedom and equality for all, and the hope of a sane and happy world.

Faith is a belief in something that cannot be proved. It is a belief in something not yet known as an accomplished fact. Faith includes a sense of possibility, of potentiality, of what might be. Faith is the readiness to live and the conviction and the commitment that by one's life and effort one can help make the possibility into actuality. One should be willing to stake one's life on one's faith.

In this sense, faith is stronger than a wish or a hope; it goes beyond them. The faith of Ethical Humanism is the belief in human potentials and the conviction and the commitment and the readiness to stake one's life on man's ability to make a better life for himself and the kind of world in which human values will be fulfilled.

The Ethical Movement is a religious movement not only in affirming the reality of the spiritual needs of man, but in setting out upon the quest for positive answers. Our position is broad enough to include many differing viewpoints. Yet it constitutes an affirmation, a faith to live and die by. It meets the distinctly religious needs of spiritual security, direction, and faith; it gives a sense of values in terms of which man feels the sacredness of life. It affirms man's place and function in the great chain of being, in the great series of energy transformations of which he is a part. It holds man to goals through which his life will achieve meaning. Through this he will make his choices, find direction, go through difficulties and frustrations, face death and the defeat of his most precious values—but always in the light of a great vision and a faith that somehow, through his awareness and responsibility and effort, man is fulfilling human destiny.

Special Occasions

This group of invocations was written for special purposes, as indicated. This one was given at the Felix Adler Memorial Lecture in May 1964.

We may never know the truth about the unknown. We shall probably never know or hold in our hands powers equal to the cosmic process. We do not cry out to the spaces beyond the stars for special favor. We ask no guarantee for human survival or victory for our most cherished values. With humility and confidence we accept the responsibility for what we make of our lives, and we commit ourselves to a faith in human values. May we labor together with good heart that our children may know the joys of freedom and justice, the serenity of peace, and the happiness which comes when human beings live together with creativity and love.

> I first spoke these words at the Annual Meeting of the New York Society for Ethical Culture in November 1932. Since then I have used them at some of the Sunday meetings of Ethical Societies and at many others, such as public meetings where they seemed appropriate.

Those who see the world through eyes and senses, who see the world of appearances only, things as they are, are in a sense blind.

Those who see the world as it cannot be, the impossible in the actual, who embrace Utopias and illusions, are in a sense fools.

Those who see the world as it *might* be, the *possible* in the actual, who welcome the ideal that grows out of the earth and meets the test of reality, these are the idealists who give us grounds for hope.

And those who see in the world that *might* be the world that can and *ought* to be, who carry the oughtness in their hearts as an imperative, a burning commitment—in them is conviction and faith.

Of such is the religion of man: a way of seeing human beings as they are, as they might be, and as they ought to be; a way of growth and action, to liberate and save and fulfill the human.

> First addressed to the members and friends of the New York Society for Ethical Culture at a regular Sunday Meeting in the early 1950s—the McCarthy period.

This is a call to the living,
To those who refuse to make peace with evil,
With the suffering and waste of the world.

This is a call to the human,
Not the perfect,
To those who know their own prejudices,
Who have no intention
Of becoming prisoners of their own limitations.

This is a call to those who remember the dreams of
their youth,
Who know what it means to share food and shelter,
The care of children and those who are troubled,
To reach beyond the barriers of the past
Bringing men into communion.

This is a call
To the never-ending spirit
Of the common man,
His essential decency,
His integrity beyond all education and wealth,
His unending capacity to suffer and endure,
To face death and destruction
And to rise again
And build from the ruins of his life

This is the greatest call of all
The call to a faith in people.

First meeting of the Special Sub-Committee of Mayor Robert Wagner's Committee for Better Housing, October 1954.

The Right Reverend Cornelius]. Drew served a Catholic parish in Harlem most of the years of his life. In October 1954 he was appointed to chair one of the Special Sub-Committees of Mayor Wagner's Committee for Better Housing. At the first session of this committee, which consisted of approximately thirty members of diverse religious faiths, Monsignor Drew turned to me. "Will you *offer* the invocation?" he asked.

I answered, "Oh, please, Father Drew, I hope you will *offer* the invocation."

"I insist," he said.

All the members stood up and bowed their heads. That evening I wrote down what I had said without preparation. Since then I have had occasion to say the same words at many meetings where the cross-section of the gathering made it appropriate that an invocation should be human, inclusive, and beyond sectarianism.

We are thankful for this fellowship and the opportunity for service that has come to us individually and together.

In our deliberations may we respect one another.

Where we differ, may we understand one another, and through our differences may we come to wiser solutions to our common problems.

May the passion for righteousness that was in the prophets of Israel, and the compassion and love that were in Jesus, be with us.

And in all that we think and feel and say and do, may we always be mindful of our kinship with mankind.

>Freedom Fund Dinner, November 16, 1958, in honor of the National Association for the Advancement of Colored People.

We are thankful for this fellowship and the opportunities for service that have come to us through this commitment to a great cause. We affirm the sacredness of every human life, and on behalf of man we invoke the human spirit, the spirit of freedom and all that is decent and generous and loving in the human heart.

Man has traveled a long road of suffering and bigotry, of violence and oppression. May we be true to the longing of those who, even in darkness, dream of the light of freedom for themselves and for their children and their children's children.

Blessed are those who have gone forth to defend their freedoms. And blessed are those who have gone forth to defend the freedoms of their fellow men.

Blessed are those who have broken the chains of slaves and have beaten down the walls which exclude and reject and separate men from one another.

Blessed are those who are honored tonight for the good they have done and the good they will do.

May we here dedicate ourselves to the task of human liberation.

May we never rest until the work is finished, until the blessings of freedom and full membership in the human community are a reality to every man, woman, and child in the world.

May we for the love of man labor with a clear and understanding mind and a fighting heart.

May the passion for righteousness which was in the prophets of Israel, and the inclusive compassion and love which was in Jesus, be with us.

And in all that we think and feel and say and do, may we ever be mindful of our kinship with mankind.

> At a dinner of the Bank Street College for Education on October 21, 1969, the large number of guests— over a thousand—included educators, officers and faculty, and supporters of Bank Street programs, and also some public officials. When the National Anthem had been sung and the lights were still low, and the guests at their tables and on the dais were standing, I gave the following invocation.

Two women came and stood before the king
And each claimed the same child as her own.

Then the king said, "Bring me a sword"
And they brought him a sword.

Then he said,
"Divide the living child in two
And give half to one and half to the other."

The first woman spoke, saying
"Yes, divide the child,
Let neither of us have it,"

Then spoke the woman whose heart yearned for
the
child:
"Do not divide the child,
Let him live,
Let her have him."

And the king who was judge spoke, saying,
"Do not divide the child,
This is the true mother."

Then the child spoke:

"Do not slay me,
Let me live,
And let me not be divided by your differences."

DEDICATION OF A SMALL HOUSE

On a high grassy knoll deep in the woods of Dutchess County, New York, Donald and Barbara Elliott, aided by their three young sons, built a home for their mother and grandmother,'Grace Elliot. Donald, an able lawyer, was chairman of the New York City Planning Commission. Despite a thousand obligations of home and school, work and community service, the family found the time to build the house with their own hands. For two years, in all spare moments, they carried fieldstone and lumber, and leaded windows, built walls, chimney, and fireplace, climbed ladders, and mixed mortar. Now the work was done.

Great buildings are begun with the dedication of a cornerstone. High structures are "topped out" with a ceremony. It was time to celebrate the completion. It was time to dedicate the house as a home for Grace Elliott.

Now, on the cloudy afternoon of September 2, 1973, family, friends, neighbors, and their children walked among the wild flowers and wooded vistas at each side of the house. Then we all gathered at the door—and this is what I said.

We cannot gather in this beautiful spot without thinking of Harrison Elliott, his career as a teacher of religion, and his life with Grace and the family that has lived here so many years. We are celebrating the completion and are dedicating the house to Grace with deep feelings, happy that we can share the meaning of this moment together.

The house will probably outlast most of the houses in Dutchess County. When in the year 2000 or 2500 some people discover this structure in the overgrowth, they will wonder what it is. For it has a strange design. Some will say, "It's a studio, a place where artistic genius worked in stone and oils." Someone else will say, "It has a curious geometric design—triangles in the windows, trapezoids and conical styles in the roof—its walls are not square but many-sided. It's a pentagon—no, a hexagon, an octagon! Perhaps it was a center for numerology or astrology."

Another will say, "This reminds me of the cathedrals, of Chartres." And still others will speak of the influence of Picasso. One may say, "It's built of fieldstone in the way they did in the years before the American Revolution." Finally, a voice will be heard stating, "This doubtless was a symbol and center for religious meditation and in-spiration."

The question may be asked, Who were the builders? Were they

professionals or amateurs? And the answers will come: The floor is level, the walls and windows are vertical, and the stone is well mortared. But anyone with insight must know that the house shows traces of the logic of a lawyer and the designs of a planner, an urban planner, and even a touch of middle-class thinking—it must have been made by amateurs. But whoever they were, they made a house that is strong and powerful. It will stand against rain, snow, and hail, against hurricanes and tornadoes. And it is beautiful, with a dignity and grace of its own.

Why did they build it? Surely, not for money. From the looks of it, it has the mark of being built by love. When people build with hands and heads and hearts, the house will last. For with love they can carry heavy rocks and build strong walls. As it says in the Old Testament, Jacob could carry impossible burdens because of the love he bore Rachel. He could wait for seven years and it seemed but a day for the love he bore her.

Grace, we dedicate this gift of love to you. May you feel at home in it. May it keep you warm in cold weather. May the cool breezes refresh you in summer. May the rays of the sun dance on the leaves of the trees and shine golden through these lovely windows. May the silver light of the moon and the gentle steadfast stars shine down upon you at night in your sleep. May the birdsongs and the steady singing of the creek and the gentle breeze through the branches bring you music. And may all this give ever more meaning to this piece of earth, this lovely site of nature, here in Milan Hollow. May you enjoy the memories of many years of gardening, music and poetry, the laughter of children, and the kindness and love of human beings who care for each other.

We dedicate this home to you, Grace. We do so with wishes that you may find health and strength, peace and happiness here. We do so with marvel for your sense of values and your courage. We do so out of our faith in life and on behalf of the many who respect and love you.

By the way, for the record, the house isn't perfect!

Invocation to the Young

Your life is a seed for the growths of tomorrow,
This is the springtime, the season for plowing and
   sowing
That the earth may green with growing for a rich
   harvest.
May the good earth nourish you,
May you never lose touch with the living powers
   of earth
Or the warm companionship of others.
May the arts nourish your spirit
And the challenges of life sharpen your powers of
   mind and heart.
May you never lose the sense of your own worth.

May you always have faith in your creativity
And may you grow in the power to love and be
   loved
And may the cup of your life be filled to
   overflowing.

The Most Important Truth

The occasion was a birthday party for a thirteen-year-old boy. His .uncle—whom I did not know—telephoned to ask if I would write a statement that could be read aloud at the party. This is what I wrote.

When you look for truth, then there is truth in you. If there is not truth in you, you will never know the meaning of truth. The wisest of human beings have always said: Know yourself. That's the most important truth.

If you love beauty and travel all over the world, you must have beauty within yourself, otherwise you will never find it, and if you find it you will never know it—even when looking at it.

But the most precious of all, you will need love. Love is deeper than truth and deeper than beauty. You must be loving if you want love. You must give love if you want to be loved. There is no magic or miracle that can make life good or change water into wine.

And in all the days and nights of your life, when your heart beats steadily and your lungs breathe in and out, you must never give up seeking truth and beauty and the decency in yourself and others.

What We Owe . . .

We are all of one life,
We share a common origin and a common destiny.
Whatever there is in life of good or evil,
We are of it together.
There is enough of suffering and waste in the
    world,
Every life is precious.
We owe it to one another
    To make life sweet, not bitter.